# 1,001 Ways to Live in the Moment

# 1,001 Ways to Live in the Moment

by Barbara Ann Kipfer

CHRONICLE BOOKS

SAN FRANCISCO

**1,001 Ways to Live in the Moment**
Barbara Ann Kipfer

First published in the United States in 2009 by
Chronicle Books LLC.

First published in the United Kingdom and Ireland in
2009 by Duncan Baird Publishers Ltd., Sixth Floor,
Castle House, 75–76 Wells Street, London W1T 3QH.

Copyright © Duncan Baird Publishers 2009
Text copyright © Duncan Baird Publishers 2009
Artwork copyright © Duncan Baird Publishers 2009

For copyright of quotations see page 384, which
is to be regarded as an extension of this copyright.

Library of Congress Cataloging-in-Publication
Data available.

ISBN: 978-0-8118-7108-2

Printed in Thailand by Imago

Conceived, created, and designed by
Duncan Baird Publishers.

Designer: Jantje Doughty
Managing Editor: Zoë Fargher
Managing Designer: Suzanne Tuhrim
Commissioned artwork: Helen D'Souza,
Gwenda Kaczor, and David Dean

Typeset in AT Shannon
Color reproduction by Scanhouse, Malaysia

10 9 8 7 6 5 4 3 2 1

Chronicle Books LLC
680 Second Street
San Francisco, CA 94107

www.chroniclebooks.com

**Publisher's Note:** The information in this book is not
intended as a substitute for professional medical advice
or treatment. If you are pregnant or suffering from any
health problems, consult a medical professional before
following any of the advice suggested in this book.
Duncan Baird Publishers, or any other persons involved
in creating this publication, cannot accept responsibility
for any injuries or damage incurred as a result of
following the information or exercises contained
in this book.

Abbreviations used throughout this book:
CE Common Era (the equivalent of AD)
BCE Before Common Era (the equivalent of BC)

# CONTENTS

Introduction                                    6

**1 The value of now**
Living in the moment                           14
Undivided attention                            21
Appreciating others                            23
Mindful living                                 26
Self-expression                                40
Now and tomorrow                               47
Opportunity and destiny                        52
Finding calm                                   61

**2 The undeluded self**
Self-knowledge                                 70
Toward awareness                               82
Change                                         89
Decision making                                94
Avoiding habit                                 96
Mind power                                    103
Managing emotions                             107
Stress control                                116
Suffering and loss                            120
Priorities and perspectives                   124

**3 A community of souls**
People at large                               130
Communication                                 133

Families                                137
Love and friendship                     143
Hosts and guests                        150
Teachers                                154
The wider world                         156

**4 Adventures in awareness**
Attentive exercise                      168
Inner calm                              176
Meditation                              180
Ways of thinking                        190
Profound energies                       198
Oneness                                 200

**5 Mindful days**
From dawn to dusk                       208
The working day                         218
Day's end                               226
Living well                             232
Leisure time                            240
Seasons                                 244

**6 Living from a golden heart**
Goodness                                250
Acceptance and patience                 257
Forgiveness                             262
Generosity                              264

Gratitude                               270
Courage                                 272
Truthfulness                            276
Selflessness                            279
Detachment                              281
Love and compassion                     283
Sense of humor                          291

**7 World of wonders**
Mind and spirit                         294
History                                 300
Body and self                           304
Nature                                  312
Science and cosmos                      326
Experiences                             332

**8 Toward enlightenment**
The truth of the spirit                 344
Finding your path                       348
Faith and belief                        354
Beyond mind                             366

Index                                   374
About the author/
    Acknowledgments                     384

# INTRODUCTION

We live in the now, not in the past or future. Yet the moment is fleeting, so living in the now means acknowledging and accepting the flow of time—that the past is past and the future hypothetical. That "now" is where we are grounded. You cannot count for sure on tomorrow coming. Today, this moment, is all you can rely on.

Seize the moment, we're told—but to take this idea literally would be to live as an animal lives, without considered values. Living in the moment should not be confused with hedonism. Obviously, the whole notion of moral responsibility is based on thinking about the future—future consequences. The past, too, cannot be dismissed—it's the fertile ground of our treasured memories. Paying acute attention to each happening, each action, each word is called mindfulness. With mindfulness, none of these things will escape you—but it takes practice.

It's so easy to go on auto-pilot. Plus, you might think that auto-pilot saves you time—but that's simply not true. If you're not "in the moment," you'll often forget things, muddle things, or drift into behavior that actually costs you time. Anyone who's not in the moment will probably end up throwing time away.

Living in the now, for a mature human being, is about appreciating the passing moment as a fundamental of existence, accepting whatever

comes our way, whatever we cannot change—including our own aging. It's about not clinging to things—possessions, people, habits, past times. It's about being positive and not being overwhelmed by nostalgia or regrets on the one hand, nor anxieties or delusional hopes on the other.

Clock time is not fundamental: it's an artificial order imposed on the organic flow of experience. It can rule our lives, though, if we aren't careful. Time management is a discipline in itself—how to prioritize, how to be efficient. Striving for efficiency is to be admired, perhaps, but something important can be lost in the process. To be driven by clock time is to lose our freedom—the freedom to be ourselves: this is what living in the now is all about. We can only be ourselves if we ignore artificial demands—other than those we accept willingly.

Modern communications technology puts pressures on us, too. To the pressure of the clock, add the pressure of e-mails and cell phones. There's an instantaneousness and a convenience about both these technologies that make them seductive. But again they imprison us. They conspire to steal our independence. And living in the moment is very much about independence.

It's also about "awareness"—an important word, which many people use these days in preference to "mindfulness." Awareness means being fully awake and alert—these are obviously necessary

qualities for experiencing life to the full. The thieves of awareness are various forms of delusion—for example, the notion that we are supremely important, or supremely intelligent; or, conversely, the notion that we are worthless, or incapable of achievement, or uninteresting. Emotions cloud our awareness, too. To be aware is to be an observer of what happens inside and outside us, and on the interface between the two.

Another thief of awareness is habit. We cannot be fully awake if we are controlled by our habits—our addictions to repeated patterns of behavior. These are shackles that hobble us—sometimes without our even being aware of it.

To be fully aware, we need to be capable of stillness. We need to know what it means just to be, and in order to know this we have to be able just to sit quietly and register the sensations that impinge upon us. We have to be able to let thoughts drift through our minds, rather than holding on to them and trying to change them. It helps to meditate. Through meditation we can find a deep stillness of spirit. Yoga and tai chi, and other energy disciplines, can also be very beneficial. As you practice mindfulness during everyday activities, you'll breathe more deeply and see more wonders. You'll likely become more insightful, more content, and maybe more trusting.

Taken further, awareness shades into enlightenment. In speaking of this, we are entering the realm of the spiritual. This is a subject on which words are notoriously inadequate, because they belong to the realm of reason, of intellect, rather than the realm of experience. It's possible to have a pure experience of Oneness—the underlying unity of all there is. But only by metaphor and analogy can that experience be put into words.

None of us is alone, and to live fully and richly, we need relationships. We all have relationships, but not necessarily healthy ones. From a core of love we can make our relationships part of what it means to be fully alive. This is not just a matter of family and friends. Beyond that, we have neighbors, acquaintances, and various groupings of community. We have a kinship with all living souls—some might say all living creatures. Living in the now is enriched by appreciating this, and living by communal values, including socially responsible behavior, and voluntary work.

"Out there," of course, is not just other people: it's also nature, the wonders of the universe. There are everyday miracles on our doorsteps. Living in the now means attentiveness—to ourselves, to other people, and to the wonderful things that make our planet and our cosmos so special.

This is the most important moment—to be here now is as close as you can get to fulfillment. Act as if you won't remember tomorrow what you did today. Have a "beginner's mind," forgetting what you think you know and letting the world take you by surprise. What a refreshing way to live!

This book is about seeing perfection in every ordinary moment, in every hard moment, in every good moment. Appreciate, respond, and sense the bloom of each wave-form of awareness.

Give each moment your attention. The excitement of being alive will fill you. The world owes you nothing, but you owe the world gratitude for your life. Let each moment be an expression of this gratitude.

# 1

# THE VALUE OF NOW

Living in the moment  14
Undivided attention  21
Appreciating others  23
Mindful living  26
Self-expression  40
Now and tomorrow  47
Opportunity and destiny  52
Finding calm  61

# LIVING IN THE MOMENT

1   **Precious moments** The miser who hoards his wealth but neglects the more important values of life is a figure rightly disdained in folklore and literature. Trying to hold on to the moment is similarly desperate. Instead, appreciate the unfolding wealth of life as it presents itself to your experience. The moment passes; beauty fades; life follows its eternal cycle of birth, death, and rebirth. Let precious moments pass into memory, without regret. And don't spend your life in the memory-vault fondling the accumulated riches you've stored there—search out and welcome fresh moments instead of reliving stale ones.

2   **Life savings** "If we take care of the moments, the years will take care of themselves."
MARIA EDGEWORTH (1767–1849), ENGLAND

3   **Knuckling down** Spend a few minutes doing this simple exercise in mindfulness—that is, full attention to experience. While seated, empty your mind and hold your hands palms down as if about to do some typing. Now look closely at your knuckles. Get to know them so well that you'd recognize them, from the

patterns they make, in a close-up photograph. Pick, say, three main ID features. You might ask, what's the point of all this? Well, you've been concentrating on a specific task using your powers of observation. During this time you've not been thinking about anything else—you've not been worrying about either past or future. You've learned something—however small—about yourself. And you've gained a little practice in living in the moment.

**4** **Listening well** Much of the time our minds tend to drift freely from thought to thought, which can compromise our enjoyment of passive pursuits, especially those involving listening or being a spectator. As a corrective exercise, tune into a radio station that's playing songs. Take a couple of songs at random and concentrate on the words—assuming that they are in English and clearly discernible. Think of the singer's situation. Enact in your mind the story implied. As with the knuckle inspection above, this is a simple exercise in focus, and a good antidote to mild anxieties.

**5** **Don't look back** "Don't let yesterday use up too much of today." CHEROKEE PROVERB

[015]

**6**    **Observe tiny details** Get close, then really close,
to everyday objects, or something in nature you
see every day but take for granted. Use a magnifying
glass. You'll find beauty where you least expected.

**7**    **Three questions** Inattention stalks our inner lives—a distracting
ghost that prevents us from being fully alive. Answer the
following questions to see how close you come to the ideal of
complete alertness. Do you always remember people's names
after you've been introduced to them? Can you summarize
the plot of the movie you most recently saw? On a mental
map of your local store, can you locate the products you
buy most often? If the answer is no to any of these
questions, you may be suffering from attention
deficit—work at the exercises and insights in this
chapter and bring yourself closer to the moment.

**8**    **Turning point** "There is only one moment in time when it is
essential to awaken. That moment is now."
THE BUDDHA (c.563–c.483BCE), INDIA

**9**   **Cultivate simplicity** Take a page out of the Taoist tradition: aim to live in simplicity (*pu*) and non-action (*wu wei*)—a state of simply being rather than constantly doing and achieving. Living with respect for nature is the best way to practice this: observe weather patterns and seasonal changes, and value the wisdom of trees, the strength of the wind, the majesty of mountains, and the serenity of flowing water.

**10**   **Beauty and justice** "Living well and beautifully and justly are all one thing."

SOCRATES (C.469–399BCE), GREECE

**11**   **Sanctify the moment** Set aside some time and conduct a brief ceremony personal to you. Quietly meditate for a few minutes, or recite a blessing, a mantra, or an affirmation such as "I am here." You could use a symbolic hand position, the chin mudra, with your palms facing up and the tips of your thumbs and index fingers joined: this mudra is said to lock the energy within

your body. Such a meditation is blessed by the ceremonial respect you show for its importance.

**12**  **Always asking** "Learn from yesterday, live for today, hope for tomorrow. The important thing is not to stop questioning."
ALBERT EINSTEIN (1879–1955), GERMANY/USA

**13**  **Pond life** If worry forms a background buzz to your thoughts, and fills your mind whenever you're not actively concentrating, it may have become habitual. Sit somewhere quiet and visualize a green layer of algae sitting atop the surface of a pond. Imagine taking a large scoop and skimming the water with it. Gradually the pond becomes clear again. You've discarded all those niggling concerns. You feel pure, light, and focused.

**14**  **Unfoldings** Events in the world develop through complicated patterns of cause and effect. Often, it's best just to let the causal sequence unwind, at least for a while, resisting the temptation to intercede or to help it on its way.

**15**     **Shades of gray** The moment seldom presents itself in definite black and white—usually there are shades of gray in there. Take a similarly nuanced approach to life, and you'll limit later mistakes and suffering.

**16**     **The art of no** There are two sides to living in the moment. One is to see and take the best opportunities that present themselves to you. The other is to say no to any invitation or request that seems to militate against the values and goals you've set for yourself—of course, this does not mean saying no to people who ask for favors or support. Resolve to decline time-wasting distractions and dangerously seductive temptations. Say yes to the good life and no to all its pale imitations.

**17**     **The third group** Some long for change and do everything they can to bring change about. Others fear change and do everything they can to keep things the same. There's a third group: those who strive to change what they can and should change but don't lift a finger to hold back the tide or make the seasons turn faster. Join this third group as soon as you can.

# UNDIVIDED ATTENTION

**18**    **Live within your skills** When doing something skillful but intellectually undemanding, like painting a wall, make it a point of pride to carry out the skill to the best of your ability. Direct your mind toward the physical movements, and enjoy the knowledge that they are absolutely right for the task in hand.

**19**    **Quiet monkey** Doing too many things at once disperses your energy, creating a state known in Buddhism as "monkey mind": your consciousness resembles a restless monkey, jumping from branch to branch. Inwardly watch your shifting mind for a few moments. Then focus on a specific mental task or topic with full concentration. The monkey will be still—at least for a while.

**20**    **Rhetorical question** "What would be the use of immortality to a person who cannot use well a half an hour?"
RALPH WALDO EMERSON (1803–1882), USA

**21**    **All theirs** Practice complete focus in conversation. This means not only listening well but also being willing to openly share your own thoughts, experiences, and emotions when appropriate—

both giving and receiving. The most rewarding conversations are ones that involve a heartfelt exchange of energy.

**22**   **Rapt hours** A jazz pianist once berated a concert hall audience for coughing. "It's a failure of attention," he said. During the next piece he played you could hear a pin drop. If you give a musician, or a lecturer, your full attention, you're sure to stay quiet (unless you have an infection of some kind). Listen deeply, and offer performers and teachers the respect of utter silence.

**23**   **In essence** "Forever is composed of nows."
EMILY DICKINSON (1830–1886), USA

**24**   **Route test** Most of us are less attentive than we imagine. Choose a familiar street at random, and list to yourself the stores or houses in the order in which they occur. Itemize the street's major features one by one. Then walk down the real street, and notice what you missed. Express your success rate as a percentage. Less than 50 percent accuracy, when it's a street you walk along most days, is a poor showing. Resolve to do better.

## APPRECIATING OTHERS

**25**    **Encounters** Relationships lived fully in the now are richer and more rewarding: awareness brings a truer sense of the value of others and the time you spend with them, as well as clearer communication and more positive emotions.

**26**    **Blessings** Before you go to sleep at night, or whenever you have a few quiet moments, summon up one of the most treasured people in your life and mentally express your thanks to them. Summon up two, and stage an imaginary dialogue of beautiful souls. What better preparation for restful, contented slumbers?

**27**    **Journal of thanks** Research has proven that keeping a note of positive events boosts contentment, and can even raise our energy levels. If you keep such a journal, note down also the people who've helped you each day. Quote their best words.

**28**    **Formal thank-you** Write a letter of thanks to someone to whom you owe a debt of appreciation. Or, if appropriate, pay that person a "gratitude visit," and express your thanks in person.

**29**  **Cross the divide** As soon as you read this, resolve to take the initiative to heal any breach you may have had with someone you like—or love—at the next possible moment. Don't wait for apologies. Relationships are too precious to throw away.

**30**  **Fertile ground** Love flourishes in the now: it must be allowed to grow naturally. Loving relationships may wither if we project too far into the future or dwell too much on the past. Allow the love in your life to be what it can be.

**31**   **Forgive and forget** "You too shall pass away.
Knowing this, how can you quarrel?"
THE DHAMMAPADA (c.1st CENTURY BCE)

**32**   **Onward** If you constantly cast yourself in the role of victim, your
destiny will be impeded. Let go of anger and resentment toward
others, and you'll find more power within yourself. Self-polluted
relationships will always block your way forward.

**33**   **Love karma** Classifying your relationship with people can
be unnecessarily limiting: after all, the most positive view of
love is of a generous outpouring from the heart that makes no
distinctions between different levels of familiarity, acquaintance,
or deservedness. So avoid the trap of pitching your actions
toward others according to a rigorous, self-imposed social code.
Instead, trust your instinct. Your loved ones will not suffer if you
show love to humanity as a whole.

**34**   **Enlightening** "Love must be as much a light, as it is a flame."
HENRY DAVID THOREAU (1817–1862), USA

# MINDFUL LIVING

**35**   **Vitality check** Mindfulness, which is the term we give to focused attention upon the present moment, is both an end and a means. It's the use of awareness to awaken the inert or sleeping parts of our minds. Why should we bother to be more awake? Because unless we awaken, we miss many vital experiences. Above all, we miss the most vital experience possible—that of living fully, and without illusion, within our allotted lifespan, moment by moment, as reality unfolds.

**36**   **Stand tall** Take a few moments to experience the sensation of simply standing well. Stand barefoot with your feet shoulder-width apart, stomach muscles engaged, and the rest of your body relaxed. Spread your toes widely to feel a sense of connection with the earth. Visualize roots growing downward from your feet. At the same time, imagine there's a fine thread pulling you upward from the crown of your head. Enjoy these opposing but complementary feelings: deep stability and graceful lightness.

**37**   **Whirling dervishes** Sufi mystics of the Mevlevi Order, known as dervishes, practice whirling as a form of worship and meditation.

By spinning they aim to let go of their egos and tune into the energy of the cosmos, which is itself in perpetual motion. Try a little whirling: lift your arms out to the side and spin, slowly at first, being careful not to lose your balance—focus on your left hand as you spin to avoid dizziness. With luck you may notice a sense of exhilaration, leading to inner centering and stillness.

**38**    **On the level** As children we spend a lot of time on the floor, but as we get older we grow more reliant on chairs, and our muscles shorten and stiffen. Get grounded—reacquaint yourself with your muscles by sitting on the floor whenever you can. Even just sitting against the couch, instead of on it, while you're watching TV will bring you back to a new awareness of your body.

**39**    **Easy yoga** If you're comfortable on the floor, try a classic yoga pose, *sukhasana*. Cross your bent legs in front of you, knees out to the side. Bring your right heel in front of your left. Feel your sitting bones on the floor, and keep your back as straight as possible. The constant mindfulness needed to stay upright will help you develop one-pointed focus, the first stage of meditation.

**40**     **Thunderbolt pose** This simple kneeling position (below) is often adopted by Muslims and Buddhists for prayer and meditation, as it encourages a sense of centering and steadiness. In yoga it's known as *vajrasana* (thunderbolt pose) and is considered to stimulate the energy channel *vajra nadi*, which redirects base energy to the brain and encourages spiritual awareness. Kneel with the tops of your feet on the floor, sit back on your heels, and rest your palms lightly on your knees. You may need to place a folded blanket between your buttocks and heels and/or under your ankles for comfort. Feel how sitting with a straight, alert spine opens up space for energy to flow freely.

**41**     **Sweet smells** Scientists believe that our emotional reaction to certain scents may be related to the close connection of the olfactory organs and our limbic system, which controls instinctive behavior. Capitalize on the power of scents by using evocative fragrance in your home—buy fresh, sweet-scented flowers, or bake a cake redolent of spices, or experiment with different types of incense. Smell is a beautiful territory within the realm of the senses.

**42**  **Holy smoke** Incense is traditionally burned in the sacred spaces of several religions—one way to prepare it is even described in the book of Exodus (30:34–38). Burn some incense in a holder while meditating, and notice its effect on your practice. You may find yourself attaining deeper levels of calm, awareness, and spiritual insight.

**43**  **Incense effects** Incense sticks and cones are usually made from a combustible base (such as charcoal) mixed with aromatic material: those that contain raw aromatic material (rather than being scented with essential oils) are more expensive, but considered more authentic—and effective. Try sandalwood for calm and balance, frankincense to lift a dark mood, or camphor to purify your mental focus.

**44**   **Treat for the feet** Among many other disciplines, Samurai warrior training featured *takefumi*, the practice of walking barefoot over bamboo to enhance the warriors' sense of vigor. Many parks in modern China incorporate pebble reflexology paths, where visitors walk barefoot to stimulate health-enhancing acupressure points. Walk barefoot on a pebbled path if you have access to one, and sense yourself grounded in and connected to each moment.

**45**   **Right here** "The foolish man seeks happiness in the distance; the wise grows it under his feet."
JAMES OPPENHEIM (1882–1932), USA

**46**   **Foot spa** Nurture your feet with a simple self-massage: rub some moisturizer into them, then wrap your right or left palm over the top of each foot in turn. Move the tops of your feet gently forward and backward. Next, press your thumb into the soles of your feet and your arches, and around your ankle bones.

**47**   **Nobody's watching** The transporting power of dance has been explored in many cultures. Explore dance in your own way, whether that's dancing to your favorite song when you're alone, learning a new set of steps with a partner, or attending a dance exercise class or a 5Rhythms® workshop. Whichever form you choose, be aware of the way movement expresses itself through your body, and in areas of stiffness. Open up and lose yourself in your body's movement.

**48**   **The truth of dance** "Movement never lies. It is a barometer telling the state of the soul's weather to all who can read it."
MARTHA GRAHAM (1894–1991), USA

**49**   **New moves** The body's systems generally adapt to a new exercise program within six to eight weeks, meaning that even the most dynamic routine will eventually become boring. If you feel your attention waning, practice a variation: if you enjoy jogging in the park, try sprinting at the gym; if your yoga practice is Ashtanga, go to an Iyengar class. Notice the stimulating effects on your body, mind, and spirit.

**50**    **Mindful exercise** Many people exercising at home read or watch TV during their sessions—machines such as exercise bikes make this perfectly feasible. However, you're likely to put in less effort if you're distracted. In any case, it's better to reserve your attention for your body's sensations, or else to visualize the improved levels of fitness or physique you're working toward.

**51**    **Second look** We continually seek novelty, becoming habituated to situations rapidly, including our own surroundings. Or we drift around in our own thoughts, not properly attending to what the world can offer. Don't underestimate the sheer multiplicity of phenomena—and when you do decide to devote yourself to experiences, try to do them justice. There are 35,000 works of art in the Louvre. Who can truly say they've "seen the collection"?

**52**    **Home audit** Take a really good look around your own home one day, attempting to see everything with the eyes of an outsider. This is a good way—for some, the only way—to notice all the chores you need to do in the future. Make a list. Try this with your workplace, too.

**53**    **Task force** Beware of performing routine tasks on autopilot. Unless you fully engage, your mind is likely to wander pointlessly, your efficiency and productivity will suffer, and above all, your quality of life is compromised when you're not fully attentive. To stay in the moment, try the following: vary the time of day at which you do repetitive jobs, or shuffle the order of different stages, or look for ways to do things entirely differently—with different tools or techniques. An element of change and experiment can enliven the most tiresome chore.

**54**    **Notice change** In the city, restaurants and businesses rise and fall; in the country, the seasons subtly alter. Notice such things: your context as an individual is an important part of your experience. If you don't pay heed to what is happening *outside* yourself, how can you fully notice what is happening *inside*?

**55**    **New eyes** Be careful not to take your own inner landscape for granted. What you've done with your time on Earth may not seem all that interesting or impressive to you, because you're so accustomed to it. However, in the eyes of other people you may have attained unimaginable heights of bravery, intellect, creativity, exploration, or achievement. If you met yourself at a party, what would you think?

**56**    **Respect each moment** "The whole of life is but a moment of time. It is our duty therefore, to use it, not to misuse it."
PLUTARCH (c.46–c.120ce), GREECE

**57**    **New ways with objects** Notice how you relate to objects: how you pick up an instrument or unlock the front door of your home. You probably do these things automatically. For a change, watch yourself and see whether the way you do these things is the best way. Just a small change of habit can feel refreshing.

**58**    **Happy chef** Cooking a meal for those you love is one of life's purest pleasures. Invite a small group over and cook from fresh ingredients. Don't be overambitious—prepare something simple that you know your guests (and you) will enjoy. Work neatly and mindfully as you cook, savoring every stage of the process. Then take delight in watching it all disappear!

**59**   **Zen gardens** Japanese rock gardens classically contain just stones and fine gravel. Careful attention is paid to the specific placement of the rocks, and the gravel is raked to suggest rippling water. Such gardens are designed to act as a meditation aid when viewed from a seat near by. Construct your own mini rock garden next time you have the opportunity— perhaps in your own backyard, or even at the beach. Once you've chosen a formation for your rocks and sand, rake a pattern and sit quietly in meditation, focusing on the design as if it were a three-dimensional mandala. Afterward, relax and think Zen thoughts. Read a haiku or two.

[035]

**60**     **Three-way balance** Some teachers prefer to speak of "awareness" rather than "mindfulness," arguing that the latter word implies an over-emphasis on mind at the expense of body and spirit. Don't elevate the mind to the throne of supreme power. If you catch yourself being over-intellectual, or placing too much faith in logic, read a sacred text and spend an hour in the gym—or whatever equivalent activities you feel more comfortable with. Let your mind know its place.

**61**     **Quiet the mind** "Talking about Zen all the time is like looking for fish tracks in a dry riverbed."
WU QI (c.4TH CENTURY BCE), CHINA

**62**     **On the move** Think of your attention as a group of walkers on unfamiliar terrain. Each walker has a particular task. One is the map reader, another sets the pace, a third keeps an eye on the weather, another is responsible for finding somewhere to camp, and someone else carries provisions. Scattered over the landscape, this expedition can't function effectively.

Your job is to keep everyone together and focused on the job in hand. Concentrate your mind and equip it to go places.

**63**    **Mind camp** When you're about to engage in a reading or writing project, set yourself a deadline for a particular aspect of the task (assessed in pages, words, or minutes). Resolve to add a certain number of pages, words, or minutes every time you catch your mind straying. Take short breaks every so often: otherwise, concentrate exclusively on your work. Be honest in applying the penalties. It's good training to keep yourself focused.

**64**    **Be here now** "The living moment is everything."

D.H. LAWRENCE (1885–1930), ENGLAND

**65**    **A sword's point** Absolute clarity and efficiency of thought are called "one-pointedness" or, in Sanskrit, *ekagrata*. Properly trained, the mind can indeed narrow to a sword's point. When you're reading, say, with only partial commitment, you'll be aware of a diffuseness in your attention—a kind of inner fog. But if you're totally focused, you'll be aware of nothing but the object of your study. Only when you pause will you realize how hard you've been concentrating. If you seldom experience this, you need to work on your powers of concentration. Banish distraction and anxiety, and be one-pointed: you'll save precious time.

**66**      **Watch yourself** Making your thoughts the object of mindfulness is a skill all meditators build upon. Immerse yourself in your thoughts and follow their interconnections, whether logical or associative. Next, detach yourself from your thoughts and simply observe their movements. You'll begin to realize that you are not your thoughts, and therefore you need not be ruled by them. They are ephemeral, and you can choose to ignore them—the first step to self-mastery.

**67**      **Basic breathing** Many of us take breaths that are too shallow: simply bringing attention to our breathing can slow and deepen it. If you find this comfortable, imagine your in-breath has three parts: breathe deep into your belly, then widely into your ribs and mid-back, then "top up" by breathing into your chest. Exhale slowly, and repeat.

**68**    **Next level** Sit comfortably. Breathe in and out, at first naturally, then more slowly and deeply. Count your breaths: first three slow counts in, and three out; then five each way. Continue this for about five minutes, gently bringing your attention back to counting the breath every time your thoughts stray.

**69**    **Deepen concentration** *Dharana*, the sixth of the yoga philosopher Patanjali's eight limbs of yoga, involves gently holding the focus of attention in a single direction. Choose a stable object, sit facing opposite it, and focus your mind on it. The purer your concentration becomes, the more distractions and anxieties will fade. Once you're more experienced, change your focus to an image of this object in your mind's eye.

**70**    **Fellow travelers** Try a group meditation: sit in a circle, and place a small lit candle in front of each person. Nominate someone to lead the meditation and keep an eye on the time. Stay quiet and be motionless in respect for others, sense the energy of those around you, and know that they're sharing your journey inward into stillness.

## SELF-EXPRESSION

**71**    **Fire in your belly** In both Chinese and Japanese healing philosophies, the *tan tien*, which is about three finger-widths below the navel and two finger-widths behind this point, is viewed as our seat of internal power. Any Japanese master— whether of calligraphy, swordsmanship, the tea ceremony, or martial arts—is believed to be acting from here. Next time you're involved in a creative pursuit, try to initiate each breath and action from this powerful "fire in your belly." Its energy will feed your ideas and help you to digest and deliver them effectively.

**72**  **Orange revolution** The Indian healing tradition talks of our having seven main *chakras* (centers of subtle energy) in the body. The second of these is known as the sacral, or *swadhistana*, chakra. Located in the lower abdominal area, it's believed to be the seat of creativity and mental flexibility. Sit quietly and focus your mind on this region. Imagine it flooded with the vibrant and energizing color orange, traditionally associated with this chakra. Then visualize this orange energy swirling randomly within you. Feel it stirring up your creative powers, boosting your ability to come up with fresh ideas, and encouraging you to go with the flow in your everyday life.

**73**  **Speech!** Public speaking expresses the whole self, and makes many of us fearful for this reason. To overcome anxiety, breathe slowly and deeply before you begin, and tell yourself: "I'm in control, I can shape this occasion as I wish it to be." If it's a speech at a wedding or other festive occasion, remember that everyone is on your side. Enjoy the power to entertain. You have the privilege of an audience, so relish the moment.

**74**   **Blast of sound** In any situation, it can be tricky to find quite the right words to express yourself. Free yourself from this feeling of restriction by taking a few minutes on your own to speak in gibberish. Yes, gibberish! Let go of expectations about what should, or shouldn't, come out of your mouth and just allow yourself to make random sounds, like a child learning to speak. Setting aside logic and meaning can feel challenging at first, but keep going—the end-result will often be a feeling of real lightness and liberation.

**75**   **Birch glade** In Celtic symbolism, the birch tree represents new beginnings: babies' cradles were made of birchwood, and bundles of birch were used to sweep the house at the Celtic new year. Birch also has strong fertility connections: the tree was often used as a maypole, and, according to Scottish folklore, a cow herded with a birch stick would give birth to a healthy calf. When you next encounter a creative block, go sit under a birch tree: touch its trunk, pick up a fallen leaf. Or just look at a picture of a birch in a book. Tune into the tree's ancient symbolism: allow it to cleanse you of the old, and inspire you with the new.

**76**    **Divine work** "Humanity, full of creative possibilities, is God's work. Humanity is called upon to assist God. Humanity is called to co-create with God."

HILDEGARD OF BINGEN (1098–1179), GERMANY

**77**    **You-nique** Sometimes when we're trying to be creative, it can feel like we're stuck in a rut of ideas that others have already had before us. Remind yourself that nothing we come up with or create is, in itself, truly original, since all we can offer are individual expressions of universal ideas. What counts is our unique spin on things. Get to know your own inner voice and don't be afraid to express it. Once you achieve this authenticity, everything you do will be fresh and special!

**78**    **Hey presto!** Metaphors and similes are the most instantaneous way available to us for creating an imaginative effect. It's no accident that this is a frequent device in poetry. However, it's also a highly creative way of looking at the world in general—it can enrich your perceptions and your conversation. Look out for similarities and express them to yourself or others. You might

imagine that a thought is like a cloud, or a
smile is like a promise, or a kiss is like a butterfly,
landing on your lips and then taking off again.
Make metaphor an essential part of your perceptions.

**79**  **Jottings** In the modern age, many writers use a word-processing
program, and in the process miss the joy of handwriting—a craft
that conjures thought to word intimately, via the medium of hand
on paper. Keep a notebook and fill it with your scribbles—relish
untidiness, in the knowledge that the brain's serendipity is a
major creative strength.

**80**  **Unsought wisdom** "Write down the thoughts of the moment.
Those that come unsought for are commonly the most valuable."
FRANCIS BACON (1561–1626), ENGLAND

**81**  **Morning pages** Before you do anything else when you get up
in the morning, spend five minutes writing. Don't allow yourself
to pause for thought, or the flow will be disrupted.
And don't read over what you've written, as you

may start to judge or worry about its content. Simply cleanse your mind of any potential "clutter" that may hinder your full enjoyment of the rest of your day—just as taking your daily shower cleanses your physical body.

**82**  **Inspiration** "Fill your paper with the breathings of your heart."

WILLIAM WORDSWORTH (1770–1850), ENGLAND

**83**  **Brainstorm** When you need a fresh approach to a problem or project, sit down with a blank sheet of paper and a pen, set a timer for five minutes, and brainstorm. Give yourself permission to put down any idea: much of what you come up with is likely to be useless, but you may find a brilliant treasure there once you start carefully sifting. You'll also be filled with renewed energy and enthusiasm.

**84**   **Value your doodles** The way you draw can be revealing: even the random scribbles you make while talking on the phone can be a form of valuable self-expression. Don't discard these doodles: take a moment to consider why you might have made the marks you did. Heavy jagged lines may indicate an element of frustration; beautiful, flowing forms may suggest harmony and contentment; and so on. Being your own art therapist in this way develops yours powers of self-awareness and encourages you to value your innate creativity.

**85**   **Stop reading** Julia Cameron, in *The Artist's Way*, advises anyone seeking creativity to try a period of "reading deprivation," whereby they avoid reading anything but the most essential material and focus instead on creative endeavor. It's worth trying—though you should also bear in mind that reading can be inspiring in itself.

**86**   **Welcome arrivals** "The thoughts that come to us are worth more than the ones we seek."

JOSEPH JOUBERT (1754–1824), FRANCE

# NOW AND TOMORROW

**87**    **In and out** Eckhart Tolle speaks of existence as an endless cycle of "outgoing" and "return." The universe in its expansion and contraction demonstrates this movement, and on our human timescale we, too, experience it when we return nightly, in our sleep, to undifferentiated being—prefiguring our end. The cycle is natural: rejoice in your participation. Your outgoing into life and your ultimate return are two sides of the same privilege.

**88**    **Sunset wisdom** Aging can enable you to see beyond the world's outward forms. People who gain wisdom with age can appear radiant, full of humor and fresh perspectives, and fun to be with. Make sure you're one of them.

**89** **Grow younger** Young people tend to reject the fashions of their elders and follow new trends, which to the older generation might seem baffling. Don't regard such allegiances in a spirit of pride and prejudice. Sample the legitimate delights of the young— that is, the ones that leave your values intact. Learn something new: the youngsters may in turn learn something from you.

**90** **New tricks** "It is always in season for old men to learn."
AESCHYLUS (c.525–c.456BCE), GREECE

**91** **Recalibrate** People at the start of a new decade in their life often feel more youthful than people at the end—to be 51 can seem more promising than being 49. Divide up your age into different units (for example, 7s) to rid yourself of this delusion as you approach a decade's end. Think of your life as a continuum. The only landmarks are the ones you create for yourself.

**92**   **Selfless** *Anicca*, the impermanence of all things, is a key
concept in Buddhist teachings. Life embodies this in our aging,
in the cycle of life, death, and rebirth (*samsara*), and in our
experience of loss. Much of our suffering (*dukha*) stems
from denying *anicca* and clinging to the impermanent as
if it's going to last forever. Don't view age like this: let the
years pass away, like rain into the earth.

**93**   **Sands of time** To instill awareness of *anicca*, Tibetan
Buddhists create intricate sand mandalas, which are then ritually
destroyed. The sand is collected in a glass vessel, and released
back into nature by being poured into a lake or stream. Inscribe
an intricate sand mandala next time you're on the beach as the
tide is coming in. Meditate on time as the tide washes over your
design: vow to accept the passing moments as they occur.

**94**   **Empty form** "Form does not differ from emptiness; emptiness
does not differ from form. That which is form is emptiness; that
which is emptiness, form."
THE HEART SUTRA (c.550–c.350BCE), INDIA

**95** **Fountain of youth** Herodotus, the ancient Greek historian, wrote about a fountain in Ethiopia that kept the country's inhabitants youthful—indeed, the search for eternal youth is as old as humankind itself. Feed your internal fountain of youth: the body's slowdown is inexorable, but you can hang on to your youthful attitudes toward change, new ideas, and new technology—and to the sense of potential that drives an active life. It can be enjoyable to take younger folk by surprise from time to time with remarks they wouldn't expect from you—think of this as splashing them with drops from your fountain of youth. Remember, too, that through exercise and good diet you can prolong the body's capabilities; and by keeping the mind endlessly engaged, you can extend your mental capacities, too.

**96**　**Countdown** "So teach us to number our days, that we may apply our hearts unto wisdom."

PSALMS 90:12

**97**　**Ageless thinking** According to United Nations figures, by the year 2050 one in five people on the planet will be aged 60 or over—an increase of more than a billion. Cross-generational friendship is thus all the more valuable. Practice the art of ageless thinking at every opportunity, with regard to both yourself and others. Let go of conventional notions of how older people are "supposed" to act: be yourself and let others be themselves.

**98**　**Benefits of hindsight** "Life can only be understood backward, but it must be lived forward."

SØREN KIERKEGAARD (1813–1855), DENMARK

## OPPORTUNITY AND DESTINY

**99**     **Act now** "I do not believe in a fate that falls on men however they act; but I do believe in a fate that falls on men *unless* they act."

ATTRIBUTED TO G.K. CHESTERTON (1874–1936), ENGLAND

**100**     **Wheel of fortune** Risks are part of life, and we're at the mercy of one every time we start a new job or a new relationship, go on a journey, or even on vacation. Don't be so risk-averse that you end up impoverishing your experiences, restricting yourself to comfortable mediocrity. Assess the risks as they take shape in your mind, then decide which ones to accept. As the old proverb says, "The fruits of timidity are neither loss nor gain." Disappointments are preferable to regrets.

**101**     **Self-reliance** "Chance never helps those who do not help themselves."

SOPHOCLES (c.496–406BCE), GREECE

**102**     **Embracing emptiness** When we contemplate the future, its lack of known features is often the thing that makes us apprehensive.

But to think of the future as a yawning void is delusional: we may not know what's going to happen, but we can be sure that something is. Never think of the future as a desert: it's a garden in bloom that you haven't seen yet.

**103**  **Setting sail** "We do not discover new lands without consenting to lose sight of the shore for a very long time."
ANDRÉ GIDE (1869–1951), FRANCE

**104**  **Safe thrills** The excitements of speed and height depend on an adrenaline rush, but this can always be achieved without sacrificing safety. You owe it to your loved ones, and yourself, to take due precautions.

**105**  **Careful living** Mediocrity may be dull, but that doesn't mean the Middle Way is dull—that is, a careful course charted between extremes. Reckless behavior may be superficially attractive, but on closer examination it offers no emotional center, no place from which to give and receive love and wisdom. Stay grounded.

**106**   **The incredible journey** We can't ask to be reborn as someone different, so we must all act within the parameters of our personality and life-situation to some extent. Even so, there are countless opportunities to make choices and modify our fate in creative ways—even to change the way we think. Visualize yourself not as a salmon en route upstream to its inevitable end, but as a creative artist, working with the raw materials of a life.

**107**   **Useful limits** Poets know the way that the constraints in a situation—in their case, having to find the rhymes—can be turned to advantage. Approach life the same way. Assess the limitations you face, and work out how to capitalize on them.

**108**   **Joy in being** "The summit of happiness is reached when a person is ready to be what he is."
ERASMUS (c.1466–1536), NETHERLANDS

**109**   **Shared pathways** Our destiny is the path we pursue with passion. For some it may be a special excellence, achievable only by nurturing a skill. Others may choose a more universal experience, such as homemaking. Avoid the common pitfall of believing that unusual ambitions are worth more than those we share. To devote one's life to living well is the worthiest of endeavors.

**110    Coincidences** Delight in the positive coincidences in life, such as an old friend calling just as you were thinking of them. The psychologist Carl Jung called these coincidences "synchronicity" and related them to the collective unconscious, suggesting that we're more connected to each other than we might think.

**111    Hand of protection** The hand-shaped Hamsa is a traditional symbol of protection in both Jewish and Islamic cultures—an eye in the middle represents immunity from the "evil eye." It's often painted on the walls of homes or worn as a lucky charm. If the Hamsa symbol resonates with you, carry it at times of potential vulnerability—whether as an amulet, or visualized in your mind.

**112    As one door closes ...** Don't waste time dwelling on what might have happened if you'd taken a different path through life.

You'll never know. You do, on the other hand, have the chance to find out what will happen today if you keep moving forward, choosing each new direction with care and a positive attitude.

**113**  **Satisfaction** "Happy is the man who can only do one thing; in doing it, he fulfills his destiny."
JOSEPH JOUBERT (1754–1824), FRANCE

**114**  **Secret entrance** Opportunities love disguises. They may even dress themselves up as problems … or, sometimes, as burdens. Look at all unexpected situations from all angles—from one viewpoint out of the many available you may well glimpse that inviting open door.

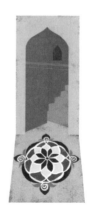

**115**  **Misguided** "Opportunities fly by while we sit regretting the chances we have lost, and the happiness that comes to us we heed not, because of the happiness that is gone."
JEROME K. JEROME (1859–1927), ENGLAND

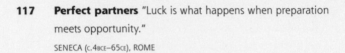

**116**  **Action time** Zen master Tue Trung Thuong Si said, "What's the good of discussing a musical masterpiece? It's the performance that counts." Be honest with yourself on the subject of when you've talked enough about your ideas and dreams, and when it's time to put your planning into action.

**117**  **Perfect partners** "Luck is what happens when preparation meets opportunity."
SENECA (c.4BCE–65CE), ROME

**118**  **Cloudless sky** Visualize life as a limitless, clear blue sky. Each rigid expectation that you set for yourself invites a dark cloud, limiting your view of the possibilities. The more clouds you create in your own mind, the more ominous the future will seem—yet the blue sky is always there. Let go of your expectations and allow the wide horizon to open up.

**119**  **Roll of change** Most of us have a built-in resistance to change, so whenever you take a big change in your stride, congratulations are due. And while you're feeling flexible, give some thought to any other changes you'd like to tackle. Why stop when you're on a roll?

**120**    **Fishing** "Chance is always powerful. Let your hook be always cast; in the pool where you least expect it, there will be a fish." OVID (43BCE–c.18CE), ROME

**121**    **One possessed** In its original Greek translation, "enthusiasm" meant possession by or union with a god. In the grip of enthusiasm, anything was possible. Next time you feel enthusiastic, tap into this feeling. Use it as a source of energy. This fuel can take you farther than you've ever imagined.

**122**  **Inspired** "Our best work is done, our greatest influence is exerted, when we have no thought of self. All geniuses know this."
SWAMI VIVEKANANDA (1863–1902), INDIA

**123**  **Overflowing** Number seven in the Enneagram system of personality types is the Enthusiast. Full of energy, Enthusiasts embrace life wholeheartedly but tend to overfill their diaries, as they fear missing out on life. If this sounds like you, take a good look at your life, and redistribute your enthusiasm across fewer projects. Deepen and broaden your attention to each of them.

**124**  **Over the top** "I must learn to love the fool in me who feels too much, talks too much, [and] takes too many chances …"
THEODORE ISAAC RUBIN (BORN 1923), USA

**125**  **Motivator** Good teachers know what keeps a pupil motivated: innovative ideas and activities, lots of small goals, praise for positive behavior, and a fun, enthusiastic approach. Remember this when your own enthusiasm levels are flagging: play the role of your own teacher by employing these tactics on yourself.

# FINDING CALM

**126**   **Inner space** To find peace and shut out the noise in the modern world, we need reliable places of sanctuary. Organize your inner space with meditation and relaxation practices—so that you know you always have one place where you can find peace.

**127**   **Green goddess** Green represents the qualities of abundance, growth, tranquility, and harmony in cultures from Celtic to Chinese. Spend as much time as you can in green spaces and notice their soothing, even healing, effect. Bring nature to you by introducing plants into your home, or carrying a green-tinted crystal. **Green aventurine (128)** is especially powerful: it calms the emotions, encourages a positive outlook, and promotes spiritual growth.

**129**   **Natural friends** The Penan tribe of Borneo know the names of hundreds of trees—yet they have no word for "forest." Take a more personal approach to nature: get to know the names and traits of individual trees, flowers, insects, or birds—as if they were personal friends. Allow your deeper understanding to involve you more intimately in the profound beauty and relaxing rhythms of the natural world.

**130** **Secrets** "Nothing is rich but the inexhaustible wealth of nature. She shows us only surfaces, but she is a million fathoms deep."
RALPH WALDO EMERSON (1803–1882), USA

**131** **Savor space** When you next spend time outside, enjoy the feeling of unlimited, airy space stretching in all directions. Air is the element of the heart chakra (see page 112)—imagine your heart being as open and limitless as the space around you.

**132** **The way to joy** "Teach us delight in simple things, and mirth that has no bitter springs."
RUDYARD KIPLING (1865–1936), INDIA/ENGLAND

**133** **Yes and no** A too-busy life can feel like an empty life, as you're unable to get the most from your experiences—like accepting three party invitations in a single night, but being too rushed to enjoy each gathering. Say "No" to some activities so that you can fully relax and enjoy the ones to which you've said "Yes."

**134**     **Companions** In the Native American tradition, each person has an animal spirit (totem) that serves as an ally and protector. Is there an animal you feel drawn to, one that appears frequently in your dreams? If so, consider its main qualities. For example, cats are linked with mystery and independence; dogs with loyalty; cranes with longevity and solitude; deer with gentleness. Be aware of your animal spirit's presence within, and visualize its protective companionship guiding you whenever you feel lonely or worried.

**135**     **Calm potential** Taoists use the term *pu*, meaning "uncarved wood," as a metaphor for

simplicity and purity—for wood that has not yet been carved has no set form and thus infinite potential. Live each moment in a similar spirit of receptivity, sensing possibility everywhere. Let a deep sense of potential fulfillment bring you a deep sense of calm.

**136** **Soul's flower** Visualize a lotus flower floating on a still, reflective pond. Imagine that it's filled with light, radiating out from its green leaves, from each separate, glowing petal, and from the bright center. Now imagine that the flower is blooming in your heart. The lotus is a potent symbol for the spirit: use this quick meditation whenever you need calm and balance.

**137** **Less is more** We live in acquisitive times: it's easy to fall into the trap of always wanting "more"—money, free time, success, power.

Ask yourself, "When will I have enough?" Let go of insatiable desires, and replace them with appreciation for the things you have. Recognize that there's very little else you truly need.

**138** **Not asking much** "Pray God, keep us simple."
WILLIAM MAKEPEACE THACKERAY (1811–1863), ENGLAND

**139** **Hear yourself think** Noise pollution can contribute to stress and feelings of powerlessness, so make sure you take control. If the noise is environmental, install soundproofing or double glazing; if your neighbors are disturbing you, discuss ways you can work together to solve the problem.

**140** **Noisy nuisances** The minimalist composer John Cage, whose works combine traditional harmonies and commonplace sounds (radio static, the sound of vegetables being chopped, and even complete silence), advocated letting sounds be "just as they are," without attaching meaning to them. Listen again to unwanted noise, and see if it's really as disturbing as you imagined.

**141** **Always welcome** "Silence is the universal refuge, the sequel to all dull discourses and all foolish acts, a balm to our every chagrin, as welcome after satiety as after disappointment."

HENRY DAVID THOREAU (1817–1862), USA

**142** **Heavy head** Release tension in your forehead and sinuses with a short self-massage. Sit at a table and rest your elbows on its surface. Place the pads of your index fingers on your temples and spread the pads of your other fingers along the top line of your eyebrows to their inner ends. Close your eyes and massage six small circles toward your temples, then six toward your nose.

**143** **Soundless joy** Of all sensations to savor, silence can be the most satisfying. There's no better way to beat stress than a totally silent meditation. Even finer, for many, is the silence over which lovely, gentle sounds drift—clinking cowbells, or birdsong, or a distant stream. Find a place of silence and one by one tune in to the sounds of earth and sky. Let stress be busy elsewhere.

**144**  **Touch type** Giving a massage allows us to absorb ourselves in mindful attention to the needs of someone else. Receiving one allows us to surrender our will, and bathe in another's care, in a blissful escape from clock time. A silent communication between two people, massage is the physical analogy of love and trust, and potentially more eloquent than words.

**145**  **Deeper than speech** "Silence is as deep as eternity."
THOMAS CARLYLE (1795–1881), SCOTLAND

**146**  **Aromatherapy** Warming essential oils or burning resins in an incense burner is a time-honored way to create a mood. Try this as an evening ritual, at bathtime or bedtime, choosing the fragrance according to the effect you seek. Mandarin, neroli, or sandalwood bring inner peace. Camomile or juniper ease tension. Lavender or geranium promote inner balance. Or as a **morning ritual (147)**, try peppermint to raise your energy levels.

# 2

# THE UNDELUDED SELF

Self-knowledge  70
Toward awareness  82
Change  89
Decision making  94
Avoiding habit  96
Mind power  103
Managing emotions  107
Stress control  116
Suffering and loss  120
Priorities and perspectives  124

# SELF-KNOWLEDGE

**148**     **Tuning in** Delusion can be a potent and damaging force in our lives. By harmonizing our actions with the way life really is, we disable this force and keep ourselves free.

**149**     **Illuminating** The Buddha's dying words are believed to have been: "You must each be a lamp unto yourselves." Absorb this energizing principle. Don't blindly accept other peoples' explanations for the way things are. Shine your own light of intelligent, sensitive questioning, and set off on your own exploration—of life, and of your own mind and heart.

**150**     **Stand your ground** Coming to terms with reality involves stripping ourselves of comforting delusions. Many people who try to confront life's difficult truths get scared and fail in the attempt. You won't gain self-knowledge without drawing upon your reserves of strength and courage. Don't run away: the rewards of standing your ground will be riches beyond measure—true happiness, true peace, true love.

**151**   **Mirror be quiet** Feeling good is worth far more than *looking* good—and it makes you attractive in itself. So if you're enjoying yourself in company, resist the temptation to check your appearance in a mirror—if you do, you may be over-critical. Why subject yourself to this distorting scrutiny? The real you is the one looking out with vitality, not the one looking back with anxiety.

**152**   **Within your skin** The world is full of unrealistic (often computer-enhanced) images of physical "perfection." Rather than feeling imperfect, consider whether you feel truly comfortable in your body, regardless of how you *think* you look. If you feel unhealthy, take positive action. But if you feel strong and healthy, feel happy about it—then turn your mind to other concerns.

**153**   **But ...** There's one word you can immediately use to lift yourself after a moment of self-doubt: "but." There's a but to every charge you can make against yourself. Get into the habit of saying "but" straightaway and completing the phrase to make a full statement. Then focus on that statement as an affirmation.

**154**    **Inner beauty** It's possible to be embarrassed about self-esteem, because we think of it as self-praise, which is different. Self-praise means *advertising* your best qualities; self-esteem, only that you're silently and modestly aware of them. Accept even the most positive truths about yourself, without embarrassment.

**155**    **The inner critic** Learn from your mistakes, but don't berate yourself for them. If you allow your inner critic to voice his or her opinions too loudly and too often, you'll find that your ability to face new challenges diminishes. Take your constructive inner criticism on board, then move on.

**156**    **Due praise** In group voice training, each person is asked to perform a song. Each other member of the group writes, anonymously, three to five positive impressions of the singer's perfomance, which the singer takes home as a confidence-booster for the future. Make a note of the positive qualities others praise in you. Keep them as a resource, for moments of self-doubt.

**157** **Muted trumpet** Beware of false modesty—that is, pretending to shrug off praise largely for the purpose of encouraging the flattering words to be repeated with even greater insistence. Genuine modesty does not protest too much.

**158** **Winter cheer** Certain ancient sacred sites are contrived so that the midwinter sunrise sends a beam onto a stone—an affirmation of light in darkness. If you were enduring a "long dark night of the soul," what would be your main consolation—love, faith, nature, art, literature? Understand what would comfort you in hard times, and you'll avoid the pitfall of taking it for granted when you're contented and at peace.

**159**    **True success** Doing something well, and enjoying it, is one of the finest experiences available to us—provided, of course, that you and others regard it as worthwhile. You may push yourself to even greater heights of excellence, but don't forget that your achievements are already truly significant.

**160**    **Spice of life** The anxious self finds difference unsettling, and may feel anxious in a world of countless different viewpoints, countless different temperaments. To accept that other people don't think as you do is a sign of mature self-confidence. Rejoice in variety, rather than seeing it as a threat. And where you do find similarity, celebrate it!

**161**    **Free world** "You have your way. I have my way. As for the right way, the correct way, and the only way, it does not exist."
FRIEDRICH NIETZSCHE (1844–1900), GERMANY

**162**    **Hobbyhorse for two** No one wants to impose their particular interests on friends, but it can be fun for both sides if you invite an unlikely friend along from time to time to share your hobbyhorse—for example, a visit to a nature reserve, or an art gallery. You may gain fresh perspectives that make you value your pursuit more—or question it, which is no less rewarding.

**163** **Personal myths** It's been said that we orientate our lives by a set of self-created myths. Examples might be: I'm creative, so I'm expected to be difficult; I lead a hectic life, which is why I'm often late. In each case, exploding the myth would require a radical re-think, and so it's easier just to leave the delusion in place. Ask yourself what myths you live by, and put them on trial.

**164** **Give way** Don't be stubborn: any unyielding quality in yourself will usually result from the resistance of an inflated ego.

**165** **Question time** When we need information from others, it's natural to ask questions. Next time you're trying to make a decision, pose to yourself the questions that you'd normally ask someone else. Include both "fishing" questions (open-ended ones, to which there are multiple answers) and "shooting" questions (directed ones, for verification). See what replies emerge.

**166** **Be a good pupil** "Learning without thought is labor lost; and thought without learning is perilous."
CONFUCIUS (551–479BCE), CHINA

**167** **Unknown for now** Don't put pressure on yourself to know all the answers. Learn what you think you'd benefit from knowing. But avoid trying to disguise your (perhaps temporary) ignorance in front of others—you'll only end up tying yourself in knots.

**168** **Wise words** "Do not believe in anything simply because it is spoken and rumored ... or written in your religious books. Do not believe in traditions because they have been handed down for generations. But after observation and analysis, when you

find that anything agrees with reason and is conducive to the good and benefit of one and all, then accept it and live up to it."
THE BUDDHA (c.563–c.483BCE), INDIA

**169** **No defense** When we're criticized, we naturally want to justify ourselves, but this isn't always necessary, and often it does more harm than good. You don't need to explain yourself to people who don't matter to you. And if you've been following good principles of thought and conduct, you can rest easy, even when people you respect might have done things differently.

**170** **Act natural** We all tend to put on an act in certain situations, yet this can get us into trouble when different circumstances overlap. You might find yourself with two people, to each of whom you normally behave differently. Better to be yourself, as much as you can: otherwise you'll find yourself walking on eggshells.

**171** **New world** Consider a tropical fish in an aquarium: he believes that the ocean is a ten-second swim from one glassy rock-face to another. We're all conditioned by our circumstances to believe that our lives are typical. Let your imagination rove, and find new possibilities for yourself.

**172** **Slow down** Self-confidence tends to slow people down, which for most of us would be highly desirable. You no longer need to prove yourself, or be anxious about everyday encounters. The phrase "Take your time" is an important one—it *is* your time, and it's up to you what you do with it. Don't fill silences with words: relax, and give yourself time to ponder.

**173** **Mirrored** "The world is a looking glass and gives back to every man the reflection of his own face."
WILLIAM MAKEPEACE THACKERAY (1811–1863), INDIA/ENGLAND

**174** **Core self** It's natural to behave slightly differently with different people: the relaxed humor we share with close friends would not be appropriate with new neighbors. However, if you change your opinions, or your accent, or your account of yourself to suit the company you're in, it may be that you're suffering from status anxiety. Remember, no one has the right to expect you to be

anyone other than who you are—and being willing to be simply
yourself is a crucial step toward true happiness.

**175**   **Lightness** A belief can be deeply held yet lightly worn—which
means that it can withstand disagreement without anxiety. Carry
your convictions lightly. If challenged, be persistent—but not
impatient or exasperated—in restating your position. Emotion
will not help your case in the slightest.

**176**   **Real labor** "There is no expedient to which a man will not go
to avoid the real labor of thinking."
THOMAS EDISON (1847–1931), USA

**177**   **Wide horizon** American psychologist and philosopher William
James wrote: "A great many people think they are thinking when
they are merely rearranging their prejudices." To keep your
perspectives fresh and free of bias, make a deliberate effort to
encounter a wide range of ideas on contentious issues. Read
a book you know you'll disagree with: there's no better way
to sharpen your thinking.

**178**   **Public knowledge** We all have opinions based on limited knowledge: who can know, for example, how peace might come to the Middle East? Tread carefully, knowing your limitations. Be moderate in your views, except where you have good reason to be passionate. Even then, be moderate in your expression.

**179**   **Party of ideas** It's possible to entertain contradictory ideas—to see what it feels like to inhabit them. When different ideas seem incompatible, don't rush to try to reconcile them—or choose between them if the choice isn't obvious. Be hospitable to them as you would to different guests at a party.

**180**   **Makeover** If you doubt that you can ever change your thinking, remember some of the beliefs you had as a child—about your family and the world in general. As an adult you may have to work harder at change, but at least you have maturity as a starting-point.

**181**   **Self-study** "Knowing yourself is the beginning of all wisdom."
ARISTOTLE (384–322BCE), GREECE

**182**   **Quality time** Indulging in retail therapy when you're feeling down can seem like the perfect way to rescue the moment—but the elation doesn't last long. Spend some quality time with a good friend instead: someone who'll listen to you and know exactly what to say.

**183**   **Rich and poor** "Give me the poverty that enjoys true wealth."
HENRY DAVID THOREAU (1817–1862), USA

**184**   **Essentials** Psychologists use the term "symbolic consumption" to describe the way in which people unconsciously shape their identities through what they buy. Keep this in mind next time you shop. Buy what you need, not what your self-image needs.

**185**   **Beautiful vision** Covetousness is an old-fashioned word for a deep-seated wish to own things that don't belong to us. Things of beauty often excite this urge. Remember that beauty is abundant in the public domain—in our museums, our architecture, our countryside. It's easily found in our relationships if only we look in the right places—and we can even find it in ourselves.

## TOWARD AWARENESS

**186** **First step** Stop what you're doing for a minute, and think about the following: the sensations in your body, your membership of humanity, your relationship with others, the sense you have of your mind and spirit. You've momentarily relieved yourself of the burden of habitual thinking, and taken a step toward awareness.

**187** **The conjurer** A magician once searched the world looking for a trick that would amaze everyone and make him famous. He traveled to far-flung places, where the children had never seen a magic show or a TV. A simple card trick would have astonished them, but the man was too busy trying to discover the secrets of the local shaman to notice. Often what you seek is closer than you think: don't miss it by looking in the wrong places.

**188** **Observer** For five minutes during the day, give yourself a silent running commentary on your actions: "I'm putting the key in the lock. I'm turning the key. I'm opening the door ..." and so on. In the evening, see how much of those five minutes you can remember compared to any other period of your day.

**189** **Edgewise** Your mind is like a sharp blade. It can cut cleanly through obstacles and perform intricate dissections. But it's a dangerous weapon if you turn it against yourself or fail to use it responsibly or efficiently. Be aware that your mind is only a tool: let it lie unused from time to time to remind yourself of this.

**190** **Thought discipline** Three elements of the Buddhist Eightfold path (see page 121) are concerned with our mental development. *Right effort*, the sixth step on the path, means actively cultivating a positive state of mind, which is more likely to result in balanced actions. Tackle negativity and lazy thinking where you find it.

**191** **Attention** Develop the seventh step, *right mindfulness*, by being attentive to everything both within and outside yourself. Notice your physical sensations and the contents of your mind: thoughts, feelings, memories, beliefs. Meditate regularly on your breath (see page 38–9) to help you on your path.

**192** **One-pointed** Aim to focus all your mental faculties in a single direction: this is the essence of the eighth step, *right concentration*.

Work on one-pointed meditation practices, such as candle-gazing (see page 180). Notice if your levels of concentration improve.

**193** **Questions, questions** Curiosity is not one of the classic virtues, but it's a sign of mental and imaginative engagement with life— and a cornerstone of creativity. Stay curious: you'll never have time to be bored.

**194** **Spring of awareness** Silence is the nurturing ground of the soul. If you can achieve a quality of true silence in your life, awareness will bubble up like spring water from the earth.

**195** **Infinite** "Nothing in all creation is so like God as stillness." MEISTER ECKHART (c.1260– c.1328), GERMANY

**196** **Surf's up** Surfers say that the ocean is their greatest teacher. Like the ocean, awareness will throw surprises our way—swirling undercurrents, peaks, and troughs. Be courageous—and patient. Mastery and balanced equilibrium will come if you're willing to learn this new skill.

**197** **Off-balance** "A mind which is not protected by mindfulness is as helpless as a blind man walking over uneven ground without a guide."

THE BUDDHA (c.563–c.483BCE), INDIA

**198** **Action plan** Awareness can be helped by movement: being sedentary can often encourage daydreaming (unless you're meditating). Instead of taking the elevator, make a habit of walking up the stairs. You might even choose to treat this as a meditative exercise, and silently repeat a mantra to yourself as you climb upward.

**199** **Think for yourself** Don't automatically echo another person's general grumble, whether it's about the weather, the government, or the price of fish. Take the time to think through your opinions, and base your response on them, sincerely. However, a well-judged silence can be no less sincere than taking issue with a grumble you don't agree with.

**200** **Luck audit** Ask yourself how fortunate you are in the following respects: time in history, place in the world, family and friends, health and well-being, meaning in your life. Carry the awareness of your luck with you wherever you go.

**201** **Q&A** "Judge a man by his questions rather than by his answers."
VOLTAIRE (1694–1778), FRANCE

**202** **True reason** Always know *why* you're doing something: if there's no reason you can think of, it could be habit that's motivating you. Now might be a good time to look at your actions, and ensure that they're truly voluntary.

**203** **Heartfelt** "Wherever you go, go with all your heart."
CONFUCIUS (551–479BCE), CHINA

**204**  **New day** According to meditation teacher Anthony de Mello, many of us live our lives asleep: we work, love, think, act, and talk in perpetual slumber. Being awoken is not pleasant, so a wise guru will always leave you to open your eyes yourself.

**205**  **Reveille** "The fool sleeps as if he were already dead, but the master is awake and he lives forever. He watches. He is clear." THE DHAMMAPADA (c.1ST CENTURY BCE), INDIA

**206**  **Fictions** Thought is a dialogue with yourself, adding a personal spin to experience. Be aware that what your thoughts add to a situation is not the truth of the matter, but a fiction influenced by your experiences and personality. These fictions can never penetrate ultimate truths—we need love and awareness for that.

**207**  **Love and peace** Living in awakened awareness is a little like being in love, when the boundaries between self and loved one disappear. Awareness removes the boundaries between all of us—yet our sense of self is enhanced. An awakened person is deeply tranquil, but has a zestful appreciation of life's wonders.

# CHANGE

**208**   **Shaping life** "The universe is transformation; our life is what our thoughts make it."
MARCUS AURELIUS (121–180), ROME

**209**   **Ancient quest** Alchemy is the art of turning base metals into gold—which, metaphorically, is what we do when we set out on a path of positive change, especially when dealing with personality issues. There's no record of any alchemist achieving the desired transformation. But in the realm of the self you have better prospects. Time can be heavy as lead ... or be converted to brilliant gold if you can tune into awareness. The alchemist's mantra was *Solve et coagula*, meaning "Purify and integrate." What better motto for a rewarding life?

**210**   **Bridge of change** Big moments of change are to some extent artificial:

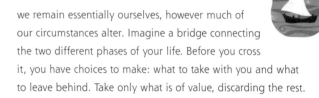

we remain essentially ourselves, however much of our circumstances alter. Imagine a bridge connecting the two different phases of your life. Before you cross it, you have choices to make: what to take with you and what to leave behind. Take only what is of value, discarding the rest.

**211**     **The voyage** "You must live in the present, launch yourself on every wave, find your eternity in each moment."
HENRY DAVID THOREAU (1817–1862), USA

**212**     **Journey planner** Look back five years. Identify the changes already under way that you'd like to continue; any wrong turnings; and the routes, so far untraveled, that you'd like to explore in the future. Plan your journey and set out—hopefully.

**213**     **Effects** "What we achieve inwardly will change outer reality."
PLUTARCH (c.46–c.120), GREECE/ROME

**214**     **Faith in change** Martin Luther King, Jr., once said: "Faith is taking the first step even when you don't see the whole staircase."

While it's important for some plans to be well thought-out, leave room for courageous spontaneity.

**215** **Start here** "If you desire a glorious future, transform the present."

PATAÑJALI (c.2ND CENTURY CE), INDIA

**216** **Room for growth** Snakes shed their skin at regular intervals to allow for growth and evict parasites. When you recognize deep down that a change is necessary, don't cling to useless patterns just because they are comfortable. Allow your former self to slough away naturally, leaving a brighter, healthier you.

**217** **Sneaky** It's pointless to try to transform your *self*—instead, it's more realistic to transform what you do. This will lead to changes in the way you see the world, and before you know it, you'll feel renewed. This technique, metamorphosis by stealth, is far more likely to succeed than declaring that you'll be different in the future—however sincere that declaration may be.

**218**   **Imperial gifts** Think of the generative power of nature—the way new life is conjured from seeds and other small beginnings. Then turn your mind to the power of your own thoughts, which is no less astonishing. You have the infinite capacity to spin one idea out of another. You are the emperor of the realm of thought— as potentially powerful as anyone who ever lived.

**219**   **Side-stepping** "Parallax" is the term for the way in which objects within our field of view, at different distances from us, seem to come together and move apart as we travel. Every time we look out of a window and move our heads to extend our view, we are using parallax. Even a tiny adjustment gives a dramatically different picture. Make changing your viewpoint a principle to live by. Step to one side to see new aspects of any situation.

**220**   **Burning issues** Fire is a well-known symbol of purification and transformation. It represents the death of the old and the birth of the new. Magically, the mythical phoenix reemerged from its own ashes. Write down, on three sheets of paper, the three main worries or obstacles that you feel are preventing you from implementing the changes you want in your life. Then carefully set light to each one (in a heatproof container) and watch them slowly, and symbolically, burn away.

**221** **Fire temple** The Hindu temple in Tiruvannamalai, India, at the base of the sacred mountain Arunachala, is said to be built where the god Shiva appeared as a column of fire. Pilgrims travel there to worship Shiva, who frees them by "burning away" doubts and fear. Don't think of change as the loss of part of yourself—imagine it instead as a fire that burns away the miscellaneous paraphernalia that you no longer need.

# DECISION MAKING

**222**    **Thinking and doing** Decision making, for many, is a fraught process. Between the decision and its execution is a slot in time through which the voices of anxiety and regret often make themselves heard. Instead, let action flow naturally from your resolve, without a break. Or if there's a waiting period before you can actually embark on what you've chosen to do, use it to affirm your trust in yourself. Keep those mischievous, undermining energies at bay: they have no right of admission.

**223**    **Trust your armory** "Never let the future disturb you. You will meet it, if you have to, with the same weapons of reason which today arm you against the present."
MARCUS AURELIUS (121–180), ROME

**224**    **Heart of hearts** When it feels like your logical mind is driving you around in circles and has become an obstacle to effective decision making, block out its chatter and noise for a while, and tune into your heart. Listen carefully to it. You will instinctively know when its harmonies strike a balance with the underlying melody of your mind. Only then should you take action.

**225**    **Discovery** "There came a time when the risk to remain tight in the bud was more painful than the risk it took to blossom."
ANAÏS NIN (1903–1977), CUBA/FRANCE

**226**    **Knotty** Too much analysis can lead to actions that are out of proportion to the problem we face. Always consider the simplest solution first—avoid cutting a knot that could be untied.

**227**    **Life change** Major changes in life—such as moving from town to country, or downsizing, or early retirement—can be difficult or impossible to reverse, so it's important that you make your decision on the basis of sufficient evidence. Don't use someone else who is very different from you as your exploratory pioneer— what suits someone else may not be right for you.

**228**    **Front seat** Faced with a tough choice, many of us may long for a parent figure to take charge and lift the responsibility from our shoulders. Recognize that if you wait for someone else to make decisions for you, you'll waste time (and probably dislike the results anyway). Take charge—and be accountable.

# AVOIDING HABIT

**229**  **Escaping the trap** A habit is an automatic behavior you frequently perform, triggered by certain cues—anything from your third cup of coffee in the morning to fleeing confrontation. Habit impedes the blossoming of the self. Often it hides a fear or insecurity: we tend to use habits as retreats. The first stage of self-renewal is to know your habits; the second is to eradicate the worst. Some you will decide to live with—in a spirit of awareness.

**230**  **Rivers** "Ill habits gather unseen degrees, / As brooks make rivers, rivers run to seas."
JOHN DRYDEN (1631–1700), ENGLAND

**231**  **Breakout** Ellen Langer, the first female psychologist tenured at Harvard, summarized the benefits of eliminating habit: "the continuous creation of new categories, openness to new information, and an implicit awareness of more than one perspective." Habit-bound souls may find the prospect of such openness dizzying and daunting. Break your bonds and discover how exhilarating life can be.

**232** **Intertwined** "A habit is first cobwebs, then cables."
NORTH AMERICAN PROVERB

**233** **Start small** Inspire yourself: make a couple of small changes so that you feel the benefits of invigorated habits. Eat a meal in a unusual place in your home: take dinner outside, eat lunch on your porch, or sit on the floor for breakfast. At one of these meals, include a fruit or vegetable you've never tried.

**234** **Substitute** It can be hard to kick a habit if you feel there's nothing to look forward to. Is there an activity (preferably a wholesome one) that has somehow fallen out of your routine? Reestablish this activity as part of your life, and relish it.

**235** **Safety valve** Displacement activity can be a good way to unseat a mild habit (though not an addiction). Think of an attractive alternative to the behavior you want to eradicate—if this involves

you in a completely different kind of activity, so much the better. You now have a concrete way to deflect temptation—a practical outlet for your energies.

**236** **Here there be dragons** Traditional wisdom holds that a habit takes three days to form and three weeks to break. This sounds about right. You may have an iron will, and be brilliantly successful in resisting the temptation to lapse—but you must be patient as well as resolved. Stay strong and alert, and keep your weapons at the ready, until the monster is beaten.

**237** **Progress** "Each year one vicious habit rooted out, in time might make the worst man good throughout."
BENJAMIN FRANKLIN (1706–1790), USA

**238** **Golden promise** If you're feeling strong, set a date to break a habit, and stick to your resolve. Tell people about your plans, circle the date in your diary and on the calendar. Make sure that reneging on your promise to yourself will bring you social embarrassment.

**239** **Cat's eyes** We're all inescapably confined to the body and mind we inhabit, and it's pointless to wish it were otherwise. However, imagining how things would appear from another perspective gives us fresh insights that can help to break down the walls of habitual thinking. Spend five minutes imagining that you're a cat. Curl up in a ball among a pile of cushions on the floor. With eyes closed, breathe deeply. Listen attentively to every sound. What would you be thinking if this transformation were for real? What would you be anticipating? What would you be afraid of? Try this exercise with other creatures too—for example, a spider, a goldfish, or a sparrow.

**240** **Samskaras** The Sanskrit word for a habit or pattern is *samskara*. Yoga teaches that we are all subject to *samskaras*, and that these can be conscious or unconscious, physical or mental, positive or negative. Through awareness we can improve our *samskaras*, and replace negative "grooves" with positive ones. Notice your physical *samskaras*, such as always crossing the same leg over the other when you're sitting down. Do the same thing with your mental *samskaras*, and notice if you always think in the same way about a situation or a person. Gently work toward changing the habits you identify as undesirable.

**241**    **Lighten up** To learn something about our dependence on technology, and show that this is not the only way to live, avoid using electricity for a whole summer's day—an entertaining experiment for the weekend if you live with a partner or children, or a solitary meditation. Rise with the dawn, savor each daylight hour, eat food cold (or cook with gas), read by candlelight, or maybe even go to bed at dusk. You'll find this an enlightening and perhaps a liberating experience.

**242**    **Shackled** "The chains of habit are too weak to be felt until they are too strong to be broken."
SAMUEL JOHNSON (1709–1784), ENGLAND

**243**    **Starve a habit** Remember that cravings are like weeds: they won't grow where there's no sustenance. Although this may be challenging, resist feeding your cravings, and you'll find they'll back off faster, and stay away longer!

**244**   **Grand designs** Take a moment to look above eye level when you're walking your normal routes around a city or town. Notice particularly the rooflines—this is often where the architect will have expressed himself most creatively.

**245**   **Leave well alone** The most special experiences are often unrepeatable ones. Value unique moments rather than attempting to make habits of them: trying to replicate happy times too precisely leads all too often to disappointment.

**246**   **The curse of repetition** "Habit converts luxurious enjoyments into dull and daily necessities."
ALDOUS HUXLEY (1894–1963), ENGLAND/USA

**247**   **No fear** Have you unconsciously made a habit of dismissing your own good ideas, or of resisting the notion of acting on them through a deeply-held fear of criticism or rejection? Break the habit: the moment a promising thought occurs to you, immediately start working out ways to put it into practice.

# MIND POWER

**248**   **Beyond reason** Intuition, the ability to "know" something
without resorting to reason, is a mysterious gift that science
struggles to explain. Some say that intuition is our soul's way of
receiving messages that help us on our path. What's for sure is
that our intuition works best when we're calm and relaxed:
center yourself with meditation techniques before using yours.

**249**   **In an instant** Don't confuse true intuition with the distorted
certainties that emotions or desires often bring. True intuition
is as natural and instantaneous as blinking.

**250**   **Guesswork** Often we hear a mere snatch of a conversation,
or see a fragment of a scene, and then instantly come to a
conclusion. It's surprising how little evidence we need for
our imaginations to work away. Beware of this tendency, for
sometimes we'll merely be giving imaginative life to our
fears. The truth could be otherwise.

**251**   **Read the signs** Our lives are so ruled by verbal communication
that we forget how much we tell each other non-verbally. Attune

consciously to the body language of the people you see every day. Can you tell who's tense, who's open, who's tired, who's happy? Watch your own body for indicators, too.

**252**    **Clear thinking** See confusion for what it is and don't get stressed by it. To apply rational thought to confused situations can sometimes feel like applying a wrench to the screws in the hinges of your spectacles—a mismatch of tool and function.

**253**    **Bodily wisdom** Consider how quickly you recover your balance if you trip. By the time you'd *thought* about how to do it, you'd be on the ground! Our bodies hold depths of wisdom, which we often override with our minds. Relax your bodily tensions, and learn to trust your body more.

**254**    **Lifelong learning** Reviewing the past might seem contrary to living in the moment, but we can learn a lot from such an exercise so long as we avoid the opposite faults of apportioning blame and feeling mistily nostalgic. It's hard to keep the past in perspective, but certainly this is worth trying.

**255**    **Past times** The past is rich with detail, the future a blank canvas. We might be tempted to pitch our camp in the past, but beware: this will impede your self-development. Make nostalgia a treat to enjoy with friends—not a way of life. Any unfolding present moment is richer than a used-up moment in the past.

**256**    **Other memories** Psychologists believe that we select memories to "prove" our idea of ourselves: "I had no friends at high school, so I'll never be popular ..." And so on. Choose one of your own personal "proofs" and talk it over with friends or family. Allow their memories to widen your understanding of your own.

**257**    **Ghostbusters** Sometimes an unresolved issue from the past will haunt our unconscious and inhibit our personal growth. If you're carrying such a burden, write a story about the situation—use metaphor or symbolism if that's easier. See what you can learn. By confronting past anxiety, you gain in self-understanding.

**258**    **Strong and supple** Our memory is one of our most precious faculties, for it's the key to mental effectiveness. Keep your memory strong and supple by doing puzzles habitually, by committing facts and figures to memory (revising often), and by relying more on your memory for running your everyday life.

**259**   **Living numbers** Using mnemonic techniques actually strengthens our memories. To remember numbers, try the number-shape system, whereby each digit is conceived as an object. 1 is a pen, 2 a swan, 3 a pair of lips (or handcuffs), 4 a sailboat, and so on. Think up stories linking these items together, and remember the stories as a code for the number.

**260**   **Memory tour** Memory experts use the technique of place asscociation to remember, for example, a shopping list. They start with a familiar journey as a basic template. Then each item of the list is placed at each key stage of the journey. You could use a walk through your house for this purpose. Progress through the house placing an item in each location: for example, you could remember to buy soap by imagining a shiny, slippery floor in the hallway. When you run through the journey later, each item should spring readily back to mind.

# MANAGING EMOTIONS

**261**    **Emotional dressage** Think of yourself as a charioteer, and your emotions as horses under your control. They are powerful and can be headstrong, but if you train them properly they'll usually submit to your will. However, if you let them have their way, you're unlikely to steer a straight course.

**262**    **Feeling and emotion** These two terms are often confused, but there are distinctions. An emotion is an inner surge when the mind is swamped by chemicals: anger, fear, lust, envy, joy, and pride are all emotions. Feelings, on the other hand, affect our behavior less dramatically. Emotions can *distort* our reasoning, whereas feelings tend to *give a tinge* to our reasoning. Start using these terms with care: a thoughtful vocabulary can be a helpful tool in the quest for self-knowledge.

**263**  **Replay** When you describe a past emotional event to someone, does the emotion come flooding back? If so, you need to work on your detachment. When recounting what happened, concentrate on the words you're using, not the experience itself. Remember that your purpose is simply to convey accurate information, and being overcome by the emotion could undermine your success as a narrator. Stay calm: it's over.

**264**  **Nothing personal** Anger looks immediately for an outlet, and that's all too often a person—the bearer of bad news, or the official following orders. When you feel the personal response building, make it clear immediately to the one you're talking to that it's the *situation* you find so annoying. Explain as if to a sympathizer: they may see your point of view.

**265** **Out of the bottle** Emotions like jealousy and rage become stronger when you bottle them up. Don't let them explode in dangerous circumstances. Go for a brisk walk, pound a cushion, or shout in a tunnel as a train passes overhead—just give vent somewhere safe to the pressure within. Then see if you can work through the issues as calmly as possible.

**266** **Mood management** Know your own moods and make adjustments accordingly. For example, avoid reacting spontaneously to situations when you're feeling cranky. If you're upset about a job prospect falling through, avoid trying to heal a quarrel or accompanying a friend to a comedy show.

**267** **Little and large** In the eyes of some people, small-scale problems have a habit of being magnetized to each other and sticking together, almost as if there were a grand conspiracy of destiny working against their interests. Don't catastrophize—keep separate problems separate—that way, you're far more likely to find solutions to some of them. Persecution complexes are usually delusional.

**268**  **Peace** "The greatest of victories is the victory over oneself."
THE DHAMMAPADA (c.1st CENTURY bce), INDIA

**269**  **Love or fear** Our two most fundamental emotions are love and fear, which in some senses are opposites of each other. Fear is often the thing that prevents our capacity for love from finding its true fulfillment; love, on the other hand, can vaporize fear into non-existence. Love makes us move toward someone; fear makes us shrink away. Find love and be fearless.

**270**  **The blue bird** In Maurice Maeterlinck's play *The Blue Bird*, the children Tyltyl and Mytyl search the world, the past, and the future to find the blue bird of happiness, only to return home disappointed. Eventually they discover that the blue bird has been waiting for them at home all along. Happiness is not an external force: it exists within you, and is always there.

**271**   **Hence, demons!** By ridding ourselves of emotional blocks—needless anxieties, jealousies, resentments, and the like—we can find creativity and inspiration in ourselves, others, and our surroundings. Exorcise three negative emotions or issues in one super-efficient inner cleansing exercise. Itemize the three that are troubling you, then sit inside a triangle marked out in string or tape on the ground. Imagine each issue as a demon at one of the triangle's points—banish it with the power of your self-esteem, and your confidence in a better life. Get thee hence!

**272**   **The archaeologist** As you dig through your emotions and beliefs, examine each find carefully, brushing the dirt away and taking care to uncover all its features before making a decision about its worth. Don't cling to valueless, outdated junk because you're attached to it: you risk inhibiting personal growth. But be careful to keep intact your most precious treasures.

**273**   **Skillful** "The art of life lies in a constant readjustment to our surroundings."
OKAKURA KAKUZŌ (1862–1913), JAPAN

**274** **Tune into your heart** According to Indian healing philosophy, the energy center in the middle of your chest, which deals with your emotions, is the *anahata* or heart chakra. Its traditional visual form (*yantra*) features 12 deep red petals. Visualize this yantra within your heart—imagine warmth and beauty emanating from the petals, enabling you to act with compassion and grace, as embodied by the elegant deer which also appears in the yantra.

**275** **Heart songs** The Sanskrit letter in the center of the *yantra* shown above is the chakra's seed syllable (*bija*), "yam." To release pent-up emotion, try chanting "yam": sit comfortably, close your eyes, focus your awareness on the area around your heart, and slowly intone this simple sound. You can use the syllable as a silent mantra whenever you need inner support.

**276** **Bright side** Positive emotions such as joy, love, and gratitude expand our perspective on life, by pulling off the blinkers of the ego. Our minds open out, and we become more creative, more imaginative, more spontaneous, more generous. Join this upward spiral now—it's the key to happiness.

**277** **Refuse permission** Negative emotions need our permission before they enter into our hearts. Bar their entry. Why let trouble into your heart, given that all it can do is evict that more legitimate resident, joy? Similarly, no one can force you to be unhappy: you always have the right of refusal.

**278** **Immovable** "The wind cannot shake a mountain. Neither praise nor blame moves the wise man."
THE DHAMMAPADA (c.1ST CENTURY BCE), INDIA

**279**    **Sounding off** To unload anxiety, frustration, or emotional pain, focus your mind on the pit of your stomach. Slowly gather these negative emotions, and move them up through your stomach, chest, and throat. Then release your feelings in a deep groan— as if you're releasing a heavy stone of emotion into a deep well in front of you. Notice how much lighter you feel.

**280**    **Journal monitor** Write a diary entry at the end of each day, listing all your main activities, salient details about each one (who you were with, what you did, where you were), and how you felt (happy, excited, anxious, frustrated, and so on). Use this information to rate each activity on a scale of 1–7 in terms of how content you felt while doing it. See if any patterns emerge over the weeks. Make any needful adjustments to your routines.

**281**    **Empty pool** Fishing for compliments usually takes the form of a modest disclaimer, clearly inviting a riposte. Not everyone will have antennae as sensitive as yours, so don't be disconcerted when the anticipated flattery fails to materialize. Compliments that come out of the blue are in any case far more valuable.

**282** **Still guilty** Guilt tends to nibble away at our peace of mind—preventing us from living fully in the present. Follow this four-point plan for dealing with minor guilt. First, acknowledge your fault, without making excuses to yourself. Then make amends to any injured party—with not just an apology but also, if possible, some form of restitution. Then make a commitment not to repeat the offense. And finally, tell yourself that you've taken the appropriate steps and that the issue is history.

**283** **Torture not** The urge to punish ourselves when we feel guilty is deep-seated: this is why extreme sects through the ages have indulged in self-laceration. However much you've erred, treat self-punishment as taboo: better to take any remedial steps possible, and learn from your mistake. If you insist on penitence, ensure that it takes a positive form that's beneficial to others.

**284** **Making it concrete** When you promise yourself never to repeat a mistake, convert the promise into an affimation that you say out loud to yourself, or write it in a notebook that you refer to regularly. Transform your guilt into positive action.

# STRESS CONTROL

**285**    **False friend** Anxiety is a cunning enemy in our quest to live in the moment, because it can appear as a caring and responsible ally with our best interests at heart. Don't fall for its trickery: recognize worry for the traitor it is to your peace of mind, and rely instead on positive but realistic thinking.

**286**    **Illusions** It's sometimes tempting to believe that if we think about a problem for long enough, we'll resolve it—whereas all that happens in fact is that our anxieties deepen and become more disabling. Don't fall into the trap of endlessly rehearsing the same old issues without making progress at all in your decision making. Let things lie for a while: you deserve a break!

**287**    **Wasted time** "My life has been filled with terrible misfortune, most of which never happened."
MICHEL DE MONTAIGNE (1533—1592), FRANCE

**288**    **Quantum fret** A small worry can be like a piece of grit between your sock and your shoe—it causes an irritation bigger than itself. The key to controlling small worries is not to flatter them with attention. Sometimes we revisit a worry only to see if we can make it smaller—but the very act of inspection enlarges the thing. This is the quantum physics of anxiety.

**289**   **Imaginings** "Worry often gives a small thing a big shadow."
SWEDISH PROVERB

**290**   **Window on worry** There's an important difference between concern and worry. Concern is purposeful and rational: a due consideration given to cause and effect, with a view to averting certain undesirable outcomes. For example, we might shut all the windows before leaving the house, to prevent us from being burgled. Worry, however, lacks the logicality of concern. It tends to focus on pointlessly wishing that things were otherwise, or obsessing about what might happen in a hypothetical future. Banish worry now: it can't help you solve a single one of your problems.

**291    Avoiding shadow** "Do not anticipate trouble or worry about what may never happen. Keep in the sunlight."

BENJAMIN FRANKLIN (1706–1790), USA

**292** **Realm of refuge** When we're swamped by anxiety, it can be tempting to dwell on thoughts of escape to "somewhere else," where we can be happy. An external change of scene can help us find perspective, but it won't solve deep-seated problems. Far better to find an inner oasis of peace through meditation and relaxation, and rely on this in times of difficulty.

**293** **Worry aid** We all feel worried at times, but if you feel you're living in a constant state of unease which sometimes heightens to overwhelming levels, take action. Explore herbal remedies, take up some relaxing activity, or seek help from your doctor. Constant anxiety impedes the flowering of the self.

**294** **Mindless machine** Machines are not living things. So why should we take it so personally when one fails to function properly? Next time you're annoyed by a malfunction, count to ten, calm yourself, and rejoice in your superiority to that machine: you are flesh and blood, able to enjoy life's blessings. And you're mature enough not to be rattled by an inanimate object!

# SUFFERING AND LOSS

**295**   **Yes to life** During his time in the concentration camps of World
War II, psychiatrist Viktor Frankl noticed that some of his fellow
prisoners found an escape from the hardships of camp life
into their own spiritual domain, which served as an inviolable
refuge. His conclusion—that life has value even in the harshest
circumstances—encourages us, however tough things seem,
to say yes to life in spite of everything.

**296**   **Chin up** "Do not be despondent on account of misfortune: there
cannot be sesame oil without the crushing of sesame seeds."
THE PANCHATANTRA (c.1ST CENTURY CE), INDIA

**297**   **Path to compassion** In hard times, try visualizing each difficulty
as a stepping-stone to increased empathy and understanding.
First-hand experience of heartache and hardship helps to develop
wise compassion—an invaluable life skill.

**298**   **The best energy** "We must embrace pain and burn it as fuel
for our journey."
KENJI MIYAZAWA (1896–1933), JAPAN

**299** **Let in the light** Deep suffering can feel like a heavy curtain between you and life. At first you'll have to acclimatize to the complete darkness. Next you'll learn how to draw back the curtain for short bursts. Allow these glimpses of illumination to revitalize you. Soon, you'll be spending more time in daylight.

**300** **The Four Noble Truths** Buddhists live according to the Four Noble Truths, namely: there is suffering in the world; suffering occurs because of attachment to our desires; by eliminating the cause of suffering, we can eliminate suffering itself; to eliminate attachment, we must follow the Eightfold Path: right view, right intention, right speech, right action, right livelihood, right effort, right mindfulness, and right concentration (see pages 84, 252, and 354). Think about what these teachings mean to you.

**301** **Shaman power** The central priestly figure in many indigenous societies was, and is, the shaman—the "wounded healer," who in the process of healing his own pain brings relief to the whole community. Our pain can be a source of strength if we can watch it, in a detached way, without feeling that it defines us.

**302** **Living fully** "To overcome difficulties is to experience the full delight of existence."
ARTHUR SCHOPENHAUER (1788–1860), GERMANY

**303** **Formless** Severe misfortune can happen to any of us, undermining the sense we may have of a predictable trajectory in our life. Often, people who have suffered gain in maturity, experiencing an opening out of the spirit. Why does this happen? Because, as Eckhart Tolle has said, misfortune destroys our reliance on "form" and outward appearance. Spend time with such people, if you meet them, and learn from their insights.

**304** **Ghost spaces** When you lose something, the absence where previously there was a presence can create an aching void—a space that cries out to be filled again. When there's no solution available (as with a bereavement or the definitive ending of a relationship), this void causes pain. The only path onward is to come to terms with the loss, and this will inevitably take time. Let your wound-up pain unwind again, slowly and gradually, as you find new sources of positive energy.

**305** **Battling sadness** "There are times when even to live is an act of bravery."

SENECA (C.4BCE–65CE), ROME

**306** **Dying light** In the last weeks and months of a final illness, people are freed from the burdens of normal existence, and many enter a stage of profound meditation. Elderly people particularly may discuss feelings, life events, and elements of family history that are unfamiliar to you. If both of you are strong enough, spend time together during this extraordinary period. Treasure what you've shared as your friend or loved one continues their journey on a path where you cannot follow.

**307** **At peace** Live a meaningful life of the spirit, one that recognizes we all will die one day. Well before the event, it's good to make peace with this inevitability. No life can be truly aware and truly fearless without such acceptance.

# PRIORITIES AND PERSPECTIVES

**308**   **Time skills** To get the best out of life, apply some basic time-management skills. These boil down to two key principles: finding a balance of personal priorities and responsibilities; and preserving your "own time" from unwanted distractions. Time is too precious to squander but also too precious to squeeze.

**309**   **Know what matters** No one should devote their life entirely to a single priority: that could result in extreme asceticism or unbroken concentration upon, say, parenting, or work, or art. Any time you devote to yourself is time you're not giving to another; any time you spend on beauty is time not spent on compassion. Such exclusions are inevitable. If you know what matters, you'll be able to adjudicate between conflicting demands when they occur.

**310**   **Re-think** Do a major time-management audit at least every six months. Consider which routine activities are intruding into your quality of life, and whether you could shed any of them. How is your life-work balance treating you? Where are the stresses in your week, and how could they be eased? This is the time, too, to think about whether major changes might be desirable—for example, moving to a new house, or planning a different kind of vacation. Make sure that you come out of your audit with at least three concrete decisions for change, however modest.

**311 No idling** "Too often man handles life as he does the bad weather—he whiles away the time as he waits for it to stop."
ALFRED POLGAR (1873–1955), SWITZERLAND/AUSTRIA

**312 Map-making** Faced with competing claims on your attention, you might choose to deal with certain tasks only when they become urgent. Avoid short-term thinking of this kind. Map out your time to accommodate long-term goals as well: be sure to organize yourself to start work when you need to, and anticipate deadlines well in advance. This may sound boring, but the benefits it will bring to your life will be anything but.

**313** **Checking the boxes** Write a list of prioritized tasks in a notebook each day to focus your mind, with a little square box alongside each one. Check the box once you've completed the task—a simple but effective way to keep on top of a crowded and evolving to-do list.

**314** **Be prepared** If you know you need to knuckle down to a sustained period of concentration, consider what may distract you before you start, and disable these distractions if possible. For example, you might decide to get a meal ready for a short mid-task break; or you might make a few phone calls to preempt people from calling you.

**315** **Barriers** Try to keep sharp distinctions between your work life and home life, and between dutiful time and free time. When starting on a task that you plan to finish another day, set a time limit and stick to it. Take clean breaks, ideally with some element of exercise—for example, a walk to a local store. Always be sure what your purpose is—even if it's only relaxing.

**316** **Time saver** The wristwatch may be yesterday's technology, but what could be more convenient than a simple twist of the wrist to tell the time? Youngsters increasingly rely on cell phones for a time check. Watches are more efficient.

**317** **Today's work** The word *procrastination* derives from the Latin word *crastinus*, meaning "belonging to tomorrow." Don't fall into the trap of believing that you'll have more time to tackle a tricky task tomorrow than today—the reality is, you'll probably find yourself as pressed for time then as now.

**318** **Value of a day** "Begin at once to live, and count each separate day as a separate life."
SENECA (c.4BCE–65CE), ROME

**319** **Do or delegate** If you delegate a task to a colleague, recognize that they may carry it out differently than you would have. You retain responsibility for results, so support your colleague—but give them freedom to act.

# 3

# A COMMUNITY OF SOULS

People at large 130
Communication 133
Families 137
Love and friendship 143
Hosts and guests 150
Teachers 154
The wider world 156

## PEOPLE AT LARGE

**320**  **The human factor** Factual information is given meaning and impact by its human implications. When learning about any aspect of our world, try to see things from the human angle: it will make the subject more meaningful and more memorable.

**321**  **Right ripples** The Sanskrit word *karma* simply means action: be sensitive to the results of yours. Every action ripples through the community of souls—its effects more or less widespread depending on the action's nature. Make efforts to ensure that your ripples will have positive effects when they make landfall.

**322**   **Ball game** Make time to attend a
sporting event. Enjoy the euphoric sense
of community created by the spectacle, and
marvel at the amazing range of different people
united in a single place for a single purpose.

**323**   **Trust others** We are often told to "look out for number one,"
but living inside a shell of caution and safety could become very
lonely. Open your heart and trust others. When someone pays
you a compliment or says "I love you," sense the good intention
behind the statement, and repay it gratefully.

**324**   **Be a true friend** If someone in your life has an annoying habit,
such as lateness or untidiness, step out of the cycle of criticism
and accept their flaws. You'll create inner space in which to
appreciate their good points, and gain more peace of mind.

**325**   **Insight** "Everything that irritates us about others can lead us
to an understanding of ourselves."
CARL JUNG (1875–1961), SWITZERLAND

**326** **Chalk and cheese** You can't be compatible with everyone you meet. Not enjoying someone's company is not necessarily a poor reflection on either of you—it simply means you weren't destined to be soul mates. Keep these people at an appropriate distance: don't waste energy trying to force a relationship.

**327** **Best chance** "To be kind to all, to like many and love a few, to be needed and wanted by those we love, is the nearest we can come to happiness."
MARY STUART, QUEEN OF SCOTS (1542–1587), SCOTLAND/ENGLAND

**328** **Connections** When you're running errands, notice the people around you—other commuters, the people in your local store or at the school gate. Do you recognize them? A simple greeting or a smile of recognition can make a difference.

**329** **Generous living** We live in a crowded world, and opportunities to help others lie latent in every moment. Stay alert for ways of doing good, of offering help, or of simply giving practical advice. Live generously in the community of souls.

# COMMUNICATION

**330** **Ping-pong** If you ask a question, be interested in the answer. Only if you show genuine interest will you be able to spin a new question in response to it—that's the logic of conversation. Without sincerity the momentum will fail to build: to fill the silence you'll ask another question, but it will be unrelated. A real conversation is an engagement of mutual interest, with no awkwardness, no mere politeness, nothing spoken for effect: you won't want to stop, nor to speak to someone else instead.

**331** **Banish platitudes** Avoid saying "I'm fine" in response to "How are you?" Resist the temptation to say "I'm so happy for you" when congratulating a friend. Think of your own ways to express how you feel, tailoring them carefully to fit the situation.

**332** **Think about it** Before you speak, be silent for a moment. Allow the right words to form. Expressing yourself clearly will also improve the answers you receive!

**333** **Shhh!** "Give your tongue more holidays than your head." SCOTTISH PROVERB

**334**   **Good listener** We all need to express our opinions, but remember that while you're doing so, you won't learn anything new. In conversation, be aware of how much time you spend talking, and make space for others to express themselves, too.

**335**   **Minority report** Unusual views can enliven conversations that could otherwise be rather predictable. If you find yourself disagreeing with everyone, don't gag yourself for the sake of a comfortable time. Gently air your thoughts, however certain you are that you'll need to defend them. Disagreement, even when you're outnumbered, gives sparkle to the exchange of ideas.

**336**   **Outspoken** "Everything becomes a little different as soon as it is spoken out loud."
HERMANN HESSE (1877–1962), GERMANY

**337**   **Speak your mind** If something is bothering you, don't allow yourself to become depressed and cranky if others don't notice. Explain it. Our friends and family are not clairvoyant. We are only known by what we say.

**338**     **Communication** Relationship therapists sometimes use what they call a "talking stick" for families with communication problems. Whoever is holding the designated "talking stick" is the only person allowed to speak. This can be a helpful discipline when two people find they are talking across each other.

**339**     **Silent music** "Talking is like playing on the harp; there is as much in laying the hands on the strings to stop their vibration as in twanging them to bring out their music."
OLIVER WENDELL HOLMES (1809–1894), USA

**340**     **Jinx attack** Certain relationships can seem to be "jinxed." What you say is misunderstood, and your words fail to come out as intended. Break such jinxes by meeting in an unusual place with an unusual agenda. Avoid habitual patterns of conversation. Ask questions about family, show photographs, talk about the news—any kind of novelty may help to freshen your dialogue.

**341**     **C is for Charlie** Learn the alphabet used by police and phone operators: A for alpha, B for bravo, and so on. The words are chosen for their clarity and dissimilarity. They make it instantly easy to spell out your name and address to people on the phone, even when it's a bad line. A small but helpful time-saver!

**342**    **E-mail etiquette** E-mails can damage relationships, because they are often written in the heat of the moment and not properly checked for errors of tone. On emotive issues, leave plenty of time for a change of heart before you press "Send." And don't mix styles, being friendly in one e-mail and abrupt in the next—it can confuse the recipient.

**343**    **Twice lucky** When leaving your phone number on a voicemail, articulate the numbers carefully, and then repeat them. Otherwise the listener might have to listen over and over—a nuisance when the number comes at the end of a long message.

**344**    **Sincerely yours** Write an old-fashioned personal letter, rather than calling or e-mailing—you may find you express yourself differently. Read letters by great writers (the poet Byron sets the gold standard): often they are inspiringly vivid and fresh.

# FAMILIES

**345** **Simple luck** "To support mother and father, to cherish wife and child, and to have a simple livelihood: this is good luck."

THE BUDDHA (c.563– c.483BCE), INDIA

**346** **Extend your family** Research and draw up your family tree, then track down a relative you've never met. They may not come to play an important role in your life, but you're sure to discover something about your family in the process.

**347** **Past and present** Maintain family traditions by passing on to the next generation family customs and heirlooms—everything from your grandfather's medals to your aunt's recipe for apple pie. Tell youngsters inspiring stories about the achievements and exploits of their family elders.

**348**    **Family fortunes** Family photos are often associated with
pointless nostalgia. But why not paste your family pictures into
an online album, and invite family members to contribute?
Keep it up-to-date as an unfolding record. Who said photo
albums were cobwebby and sad?

**349**    **Down the line** Remember your distant cousins—send them all
a greeting card. You may have little in common with them, but
why not value and grow the definable connection of kinship?

**350**    **Always surprising** "You don't choose your family. They are
God's gift to you, as you are to them."
DESMOND TUTU (BORN 1931), SOUTH AFRICA

**351**    **Private practice** Find your our own ways to commemorate
those you have lost. A gift of flowers left in a churchyard or
crematorium may seem arbitrary and small, but it gives you
time—on the way there perhaps—to meditate on the person and
be grateful for having known them and enjoyed their special
gifts. You might prefer to leave flowers in a favorite spot instead.

**352** **Others within** "In different hours, a man represents each of several of his ancestors, as if there were seven or eight of us rolled up in each man's skin—and they constitute the variety of notes for that new piece of music which his life is."

RALPH WALDO EMERSON (1803–1882), USA

**353** **Family walkathon** Go on a family pride march—as many of your family as possible, tramping the streets, hills, or woods. If a wheelchair is needed, take turns to push, and embellish the chair with balloons decorated with your slogans of family pride.

**354** **Begin bonding** If you're pregnant, follow the tradition of mothers-to-be in ancient China by meditating on the new life within you. Sit somewhere quiet, close your eyes, take long, deep breaths. Visualize your tiny baby floating in your womb and imagine yourself enveloping him or her with your love. Hold this image in your mind's eye for a few minutes.

**355** **See eye to eye** Newborn babies love to look at faces, so be sure to give your child plenty of eye contact—feeding time gives you an ideal opportunity. Newborns can't focus beyond about 12 inches (30 cm), so hold them close as often as you can.

**356** **Bathe cares away** The demands of motherhood can be overwhelming, so take a few minutes each day to restore your inner equilibrium. Immersing yourself in a luxurious bath while your partner or a friend babysits can be a wonderful escape. Lean back, relax your body into the sensuous water, and unwind.

**357** **Flower power** Do a science experiment with (not on!) children. You'll need water, three small vases, some red, blue, and yellow food coloring, and three white carnations (or similar flowers). Pour a little water into each vase, add 15–20 drops of red food coloring to the water in the first vase, blue to the second, and yellow to the third. Place a carnation in each vase. As the flowers

"drink" the water, the blooms will slowly change hue, usually within twenty-four hours. See which dye is absorbed the fastest.

**358**    **Equal voices** It's easy to forget that children have their own opinions. Include them in discussions on family matters. Even if you don't agree with their suggestions, you can thank them for their contribution and show them that you value their views.

**359**    **Jobs for all** Kids benefit from responsibilities, which help their self-esteem. Charge a child with the task of remembering something, or bringing something along, or such like—if they do well, stretch them a little further next time.

**360**    **Great kids** Children are the seedbed of future excellence—give credit to other people's children whenever you have the chance.

**361**  **Share your skills** If you speak a second language or play a musical instrument, teach it to a child or a group of young people. Sharing your skills is one of life's great pleasures.

**362**  **Teen work** Enlighten a teenager by giving him or her advice or information you'd like to have had when you were that age. What better way to contribute to evolution?

**363**  **Appreciation** "Children find everything in nothing; men find nothing in everything."
GIACOMO LEOPARDI (1798–1837), ITALY

**364**  **Renewal** As we grow older, the interests of teenagers and young people can seem increasingly incomprehensible. Ask a young friend to introduce you to their favorite pastime. It's sure to be a challenge, and you may even enjoy the new experience!

**365**  **Wise one** Take on the mantle of the sage whenever you sense that a younger person has respect for you. You have the opportunity to exert subtle and benevolent influences.

# LOVE AND FRIENDSHIP

**366**   **Take another look** If you're living with someone, you can soon fall into the trap of taking them for granted. From time to time audit your relationship together to assess how responsive your bond is. In a lighthearted way, you could even award each other points out of ten for various aspects, such as thoughtfulness, communication, and physical gestures.

**367**   **Affirmations** The playwright Noël Coward said, "I can take any amount of criticism as long as it's unqualified praise"—and the truth is, most of us thrive on positive rather than negative remarks. When resolving difficulties with your partner, apply this principle, and make sure pluses outnumber minuses.

**368**   **Change of scene** Spending the weekend with your partner in an entirely new place can help you to see them in a new light— but be sure to keep busy, and fully engaged with the sights and activities on offer. Otherwise, you may find yourself marooned together in the same old way, but without an escape route.

**369** **Switching selves** When resolving an intractable relationship difficulty, try exchanging roles. Say what you think the other person would say. Freestyle role play can be enlightening.

**370** **Hangover cure** Unresolved issues with a partner can affect your sleep quality—and the next day the problem can seem all the more formidable. Before bedtime, try to resolve the tension or agree to talk about it at a specific time in the future. Or if you sense your partner is troubled yet unwilling to talk, empathize: he or she may be inwardly struggling. Make a warm gesture (such as a hug) to show, wordlessly, that you understand.

**371** **Divided** "Shared joy is a double joy; shared sorrow half a sorrow."
SWEDISH PROVERB

**372** **Breakaway** Many of us fall into moods without even being aware of how damaging they can be to relationships. In a

professional context, you would never allow a mood to affect your performance. Be ruthless with your own moods in a relationship setting also: your partner deserves better.

**373** **Be spontaneous** Inject excitement into the precious time you spend with your partner by sometimes deliberately not planning what to do and where to go in advance. Simply see how you both feel at the time and act on the spur of the moment.

**374** **The gardeners** "Let us be grateful to people who make us happy, the charming gardeners who make our souls blossom."
MARCEL PROUST (1871–1922), FRANCE

**375** **Wayfarers** The road to awareness offers a highly personal experience, but that doesn't mean you have to travel it alone. Perhaps your partner is also questing for deeper truths? Exchange insights and setbacks. Give solace during dark nights of the soul.

**376** **Together** "No road is long with good company."
TURKISH PROVERB

**377**  **Perfect peacock** When a beam of sunlight catches the resplendent tail feathers of a peacock, the effect is one of dazzling beauty. In the same way, people can surprise us when we see them in a different light from usual, or in different circumstances. Be alert to flashes of unexpected beauty all around you, from family and friends—surprising acts of courage, compassion, wit, or wisdom. Such moments will enrich your life.

**378**  **Matchless** Comparison is not always desirable. It's good when you're making a choice, but it isn't good when you're having an evening out with a friend and you're comparing them with another friend. Some experiences are beyond compare.

**379**  **One of a kind** Adhering to shared values is the essence of a healthy society. Yet we remain individuals, and the choices we make may not always be the ones our friends, family, and work colleagues would urge upon us. Peer pressure is a powerful force, but at times you'll feel you must resist it. Go your own way if you have to—explain why to the people you care about; and ignore those people who have no right to interfere.

**380**  **Boundaries** Set and respect your own boundaries with regard to other people. If you'd rather not give someone your e-mail address, don't feel obliged: just politely refuse. Or if a friend is becoming too needy, speak honestly (but sensitively) with them about the limits of what you can give.

**381**  **Close to home** If you're spending less time with old friends, and yet find that you're not making new ones, consider the people you see the most of at work or in daily life. Can you deepen these casual acquaintances? You may have subconsciously dismissed someone who, with a little attention, could become a true friend.

**382**  **Threesome** When planning social occasions, especially dinner or lunch parties, people tend to strive for even numbers. Experiment with odd numbers—even three, which some think of as "difficult." A three-way conversation can have a fascinating dynamic.

**383**  **Friendship refreshment** If treasured friends move far away, loss of familiarity with their daily lives can make you feel as though you've "lost" the friendship. Visit their new home when you can.

This will help you understand their routines, their issues, and their daily environment, bringing you closer despite the distance.

**384** **Valued** "Hold a true friend with both hands."
NIGERIAN PROVERB

**385** **Anniversary waltz** Recognizing friends' birthdays is gracious and kind. As friends age, they may not expect this—which makes the gesture even more valuable as an expression of loyalty and appreciation. Be strict with yourself: keep records of key birthdays, and if you forget to mail a card, make a celebratory phone call instead, or send an e-mail or text message.

**386** **Treasure** "True love is rare; true friendship still rarer."
JEAN DE LA FONTAINE (1621–1695), FRANCE

**387** **Truly close** If you're mourning the absence of faraway friends and family, take a few minutes to visualize them dwelling in your heart. Although the physical distance between you may be farther than you'd like, they'll always be there.

# HOSTS AND GUESTS

**388**    **Honored guests** A *rangoli* is
an intricate design drawn on the
ground outside Indian homes
to extend hospitality to visitors.
Traditionally this is made in
powdered rice, a gesture of
welcome to smaller creatures, such
as birds and ants, who consume
the powder. During the day the
rangoli is scattered by weather,
animals, and the coming and
going of feet, symbolizing the
transience of life. It's remade in
a different pattern the following
morning. Think up your own
symbolic way to welcome visitors
to your home. You could devise
your own symbolic *rangoli*—or
simply buy an amusing or
appropriate welcome mat.

**389** **Chance remark** Traditionally, during the Japanese tea ceremony, the guests compliment the decoration of the room and the implements used. When you're a guest in someone's home, notice your surroundings. Pick out an interesting object or detail, and ask your host about it. You may learn more than you expect: many features will have stories behind them.

**390** **Purify and prepare** Prior to welcoming his guests, the host of a tea ceremony purifies himself by washing his hands and mouth. Before you welcome guests into your home, allow yourself a few moments to mentally purify yourself. Consider why you've invited your guests, and visualize how you would like their stay in your home to be. You'll find that your gratitude toward them, and your appreciation of their qualities, will subtly grow.

**391** **Holy duty** It can be disconcerting, or even stressful, if a guest turns up unexpectedly. If this happens to you, remember the Rule of St. Benedict, a book of Christian monastic precepts written around 530: "Let all guests that come be received like Christ himself." Even if your guests are unexpected, welcome them with an open heart, and remember that, in many religions, having guests in your home is considered a blessing.

**392**    **Honored guests** "The house that receives no guests, never receives angels."

TURKISH PROVERB

**393**    **No thank you** Sharing is such a natural way of life for the traditionally nomadic Penan people, in Borneo, that there's no term in their language for "thank you." Take a leaf out of their book by sharing whatever you have (no matter how little) without expecting anything in return—not even an expression of thanks.

**394**    **Light a candle** "Thousands of candles can be lit from a single candle, and the life of the candle will not be shortened. Happiness never decreases by being shared."

THE BUDDHA (c.563–c.483BCE), INDIA

**395**    **The art of being a guest** To be a guest in someone else's home is as much an art as being a successful host. Be aware of your host's needs, especially the need for privacy at times. Decide how you can make a welcome contribution—it might even be by offering DIY skills. Behave with grace and gratitude— this is the best way to make sure you're invited again.

**396** **Key chain** If you regularly entertain guests overnight, or are having someone for a few days, cut an extra set of keys. Lending keys will make them feel trusted, welcomed, and independent, and it will save worry, time, and effort for both of you—leaving you free to enjoy their visit.

**397** **Show appreciation** Tailor a thank-you gift carefully to your host. Coordinate colors with the home or with clothes you've seen them wearing. If you opt for food or drink, check it's consistent with their tastes and their dietary needs. Your gift is an expression of thoughtfulness, so make sure it's appropriate.

**398** **Food for thought** "An onion shared with a friend tastes like roast lamb."
EGYPTIAN PROVERB

# TEACHERS

**399** **Two-way process** Teachers of every subject, from geography to computing to Pilates, cite the beneficial influence of their students. Many teachers say that it's their students who, in fact, teach them to teach. Remember this two-way process when you're learning something new, and honor it by giving your teacher your full effort and attention.

**400** **Insights and experiences** Teachers can seem formidably knowledgeable and sophisticated, but don't be afraid of telling them about your own experiences of the subject. Overcome any sense of inferiority. A teacher to whom no pupil volunteers his or her own insights would soon become lonely and dissatisfied.

**401** **Listen and learn** "A single conversation with a wise man is better than ten years of study."
CHINESE PROVERB

**402** **Thanking your teachers** In traditional yoga classes, before a teacher begins a lesson, he or she chants a mantra thanking their own guru, or teacher. Consider all the teachers you've met during your life, and the things they've taught you. These may be concrete skills, such as mathematics or cooking, or something less subject-based, such as how to love. Take a few minutes to mentally thank all your teachers who've brought you to this stage of your life.

**403** **Obits** Read obituaries in newspapers. The lives of those who lived through war and deprivation far removed from our own experience have much to teach us. And we'll be reminded just how individual and unorthodox are the lives many people lead.

**404** **Head-turner** A teacher can help anyone on the path to awareness. The most valuable is not the one with the deepest knowledge of the scriptures, or the most eloquent: it's the one who points you in the direction that enables you to see.

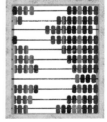

**405** **The inner guru** "Teachers open the door but you must enter by yourself."
CHINESE SAYING

# THE WIDER WORLD

**406**    **Community spirit** *Sangha* is the Sanskrit word for a community united with a common purpose, made up of people who both learn from and teach one another as they progress toward their shared goal. Cultivate your own *sangha* through involvement in group activities in your local area, whether cultural, political, sporting, or social. Feel connected to those who live around you.

**407**    **Summer fun** Celebrate the summer by organizing an outdoor party for everyone who lives in your street, on your block, or in your apartment building. There may well be a wide variety of races, ages, and backgrounds present—marvel at the diversity within a relatively small area.

**408**    **Newcomer** When a new neighbor arrives in your building or neighborhood, answer their questions, share stories, introduce them around. Neighbors can be more helpful than friends or relatives in some ways, simply because they live so close.

**409**    **Helpline** Be considerate of elderly neighbors, and help them when you can. Do their shopping, or accompany them on a

shopping trip. Or just give them the gift of company. Many elderly folk live alone: call on them, and invite them over to you.

**410** **Manners matter** Civility toward strangers is an old-fashioned virtue, implying well-mannered consideration for all around you. If you value this quality, and observe its simple precepts, you'll make people feel better about life. The effort involved is not great. Keep your poise and your patience. Be gracious with all.

**411** **The value of now** "You cannot do a kindness too soon, for you never know how soon it will be too late."
RALPH WALDO EMERSON (1803–1882), USA

**412** **Over the fence** Sharing gardening lore, and swapping plants, is just one way in which neighbors can benefit from a shared fence over which they can speak to each other. Value such occasions—and make the most of them.

**413** **Meals on wheels** If a friend or neighbor is struggling, a home-cooked meal they can reheat at their convenience can provide great comfort. You could even offer to cook something (perhaps just breakfast) in their kitchen, if that wouldn't be intrusive.

**414** **De-clutter generously** Divide unwanted items into "trash or treasure" when you're de-cluttering your home. Recycle the trash; give away the treasure. You may wish to sell expensive items in good condition, but as this would be unbudgeted income, couldn't you afford to give them away instead? Matching each object to an appreciative recipient can be rewarding, just like any other form of voluntary work.

**415** **Eyes open** Be on the lookout for ways to help others enjoy life—carry a stranger's shopping bags, buy several pairs of winter gloves and donate them to needy people, give a disposable camera to a child who's setting off on vacation. Invest generously in others' happiness—you'll discover benefits for your own.

**416** **For others** "What we do for ourselves dies with us. What we do for others and the world remains and is immortal."
ALBERT PINE (c.1800–1851), ENGLAND

**417**  **Campaign trail** If you feel galvanized by a local good cause, invest your energy generously—get involved in publicizing and proselytizing. Relish the legwork, knowing that each step you take, each doorbell you ring, is for a worthwhile purpose.

**418**  **More than money** Investigate the charities in your local area, and get involved with the ones that appeal to you. Giving just a few hours per week, or a weekday evening, could well end up being worth more than a thousand dollars in donations.

**419**  **Back the school** If you'd like to make a contribution to the future of your community, consider a local school. You could donate cash, fund new textbooks in your favorite subject, or replace a worn-out piece of equipment. Or if you're feeling the pinch financially, donote your skills instead.

**420**  **Solo performance** Talk to your local library about doing some kind of presentation there for the community—we all have special knowledge or experience, and you might be surprised by how many people would be interested in learning more.

**421**  **World library** If you've truly loved reading a particular book, why not leave a copy somewhere public, like on a park bench, for a stranger to pick up and enjoy?

**422**  **People power** In the age of global warming and climate change, we can make the most difference to the environment if we act together as a community. Take pride even in small responsible gestures, such as lowering your thermostat or recycling a glass bottle. If enough of us develop good habits like this, maybe our action will end up saving future lives—from polar bears to people.

**423** **Litter campaign** Show your respect for the environment, and for the area where you live, by campaigning against the littering of outdoor space. Organize a neighborhood "litter-pick" to wipe the slate clean, then decide as a community to adopt a policy of no-tolerance toward litter, by picking it up anywhere you see it. Demonstrate your own commitment daily.

**424** **Wrap-free zone** The commercialization of religious and secular public holidays is a familiar theme of complaint. Mount your own personal rebellion against this by avoiding commercial wrapping paper for presents and creating your own instead, through basic craft work. A personalized gift is always better received. An extension of this idea would be to use homemade (ideally biodegradable) decorations and serve locally-sourced food at your festive meals.

**425** **Swap-shop** Organize a swap-shop with friends a few weeks before Christmas: this is a great way to usefully dispose of unwanted items, and at the same time source Christmas gifts without spending unnecessary cash. Give away things that you don't need, and choose some second-hand presents for people who you know share your principles.

**426** **Rule of five** Positive psychologists have discovered that performing acts of altruism or kindness significantly increases people's happiness levels. Try to do at least five assorted kind acts a week, no matter how big or how small. Even better, try to do five in one day now and then! Or even every day!

**427** **Everyday goodness** "Always be a little kinder than necessary."
J.M. BARRIE (1860–1937), SCOTLAND

**428** **All together** Fellow-feeling between strangers is one of the most valuable characteristics of our species. You'll come across lots of exceptions, but remind yourself at such times that communal empathy is the norm.

**429** **Helping hands** One of the five daily duties performed by Hindus is giving food and water to anyone or anything in need. Next time you're watering a withering plant or putting food out for winter birds, think of it in this light.

**430**      **Caring souls** Children are horrified when they see or hear of an animal suffering, yet some of us lose this sensitivity as we grow older. Reawaken your sense of compassion toward animals, and act on it: this may mean donating to an animal charity, or turning vegetarian. Kindness toward all sentient beings is a tenet of most major religions.

**431**      **Warm freeze** We've all been "cold-called" by commercial concerns, and it can be extremely annoying. Be polite, even when the call is coming at the worst possible time. You're speaking to someone who relies on this job for their livelihood.

**432**      **Opportunities abound** "Wherever there is a human being, there is an opportunity for a kindness."
SENECA (c.4BCE–65CE), ROME

**433**      **Thank you!** People in service professions often feel invisible. Thank the mailman, the road sweeper, or the trash collector when you meet him near your home. A small gesture of gratitude could be a bright spot in their day.

# 4

## ADVENTURES IN AWARENESS

Attentive exercise  168
Inner calm  176
Meditation  180
Ways of thinking  190
Profound energies  198
Oneness  200

## ATTENTIVE EXERCISE

**434** **All-round fitness** Bringing your attention fully to each moment can be difficult if you're distracted by physical stiffness, aches, and pains. Use some of the following techniques to loosen and strengthen your body. They'll make reliable companions on the road to awareness—freeing your mind for its adventures.

**435** **Pipeline** In yoga, the central channel for life energy (*prana*) is the *sushumna nadi*, which runs straight up the spine—some practitioners think of it as located in the spinal cord. Close your eyes and visualize this channel as a flowing stream of white light. Thank it for energizing you, and enabling your day's activities.

**436** **Mountain pose** Yoga postures prepare the body for stationary breathing exercises (*pranayama*) and meditation. Try the following postures **(436–440)**, all suitable for complete beginners. Start with *tadasana*, or mountain pose, which gives you the strong, stable feeling of a mountain. Stand with your feet parallel and slightly apart, hands by your sides. Distribute your weight evenly over each foot. Check that your knees are parallel, and that one hip or shoulder is not higher than the other. Point your fingers gently downward. Softly lift the front of your body and relax your shoulders and the back of your body. Keep your head level.

**437** **Turn inward** Forward bends connect us with our inner self. Stand with your feet slightly apart and parallel. Breathe in, lift your arms above your head, then breathe out and bend gently forward. Bring your hands to your thighs, calves, or the floor. Stay here for one breath, then slowly roll your spine up to standing.

**438** **Like a tree** Balancing teaches us about inner stillness: for it's only when we're mentally quiet and aware that we find physical equilibrium. Stand with your feet together and parallel. Focus your eyes on a still point in front of you. Bend your right knee and lift your right leg, then turn that leg out from the hip, and place the sole of your right foot on your left inner thigh or calf. Balance for a few seconds, then repeat on the other side.

**439**　**Heart opener** Bending backward from the waist and lifting the upper body helps us to be open-hearted and courageous. Lie on the floor on your back, with your knees bent, feet hip-width apart and parallel. Breathe in, press your feet into the floor, and lift your hips, keeping your thighs parallel (as shown above). Breathe out and return to your starting position. Repeat three times.

**440**　**Corpse pose** After a yoga sequence, or as a stand-alone posture, practice *savasana*, the corpse pose. Lie on your back with your feet apart, hands away from your sides and palms up. Cover yourself with a blanket and shift around until you're truly comfortable, then commit to staying absolutely still, but mentally aware, for a few minutes. The challenge is to avoid falling asleep!

**441**    **Roll-down** For the subtle, toning movements of Pilates, you need sustained concentration, which eventually leads to increased awareness in both mind and body. These simple roll-downs will awaken your core being. Lie on your back with knees bent, feet on the floor. Support your head with your hands. Breathe out, engage your abdominals, and lift your head and shoulders. Breathe in, then breathe out and release. Repeat six times.

**442**    **Pilates oyster** To stimulate awareness of your hips and outer thighs, lie on your right side with knees bent halfway in and feet in line with your tailbone. Rest your head on your right arm, and place your left hand on your left hip (to keep it aligned over your right hip). Engage your abdominals and, with feet together, slowly lift your left knee: imagine an oyster shell opening. Repeat five times. Then swap sides.

[ 171 ]

**443**     **Sensing chi** The graceful movements of tai chi increase the flow of life-energy (*chi*) around the body, giving us increased strength, balance, and optimism. Stand with your feet hip-width apart. Imagine there's a balloon under each of your palms, and a weight attached to each elbow. Allow your palms to float up to shoulder height, as you keep the elbows half-bent. Bend your elbows more, to draw your palms to your shoulders. Reverse the movement: imagine pushing the balloons back down. Bend your knees a little more. Return to standing.

**444**     **Punching chi** This tai chi exercise, called "Punch tiger's ears," will help you feel focused and dynamic. Stand with your feet parallel, hip-width apart, hands by your sides. Make soft fists with your hands, thumbs inside. Breathe in and step your left heel forward, so that it's in gentle contact with the floor. At the same time, lift your fists in a circle out to the sides, and in front of you, level with your face. Breathe out, transfer your weight onto the sole of your left foot, and bring both your fists toward each other, as if you were "punching a tiger's ears." Return to standing and repeat, stepping your right foot forward.

**445**   **Sun breath** This deep breathing technique quickly relieves tension. Learn the stages, then treat it as a single flowing breath. Stand with arms by your sides. Step 1 is to breathe into your belly while stretching out your arms; step 2, to breathe into mid-chest as you bring your hands to the prayer position at your heart; step 3, to lift your arms over your head as you breathe into your upper chest. Lower your arms to your sides again as you exhale.

**446**   **Pressure point** There's a simple acupressure technique you can apply to yourself to stimulate awareness. Hold your left hand, palm down with thumb and forefinger spread, in front of you, supported by your right hand. Apply gentle pressure with the right thumb to the fleshy part of the hand between thumb and forefinger. Hold for about two minutes. Then switch hands and repeat the exercise. (Avoid when pregnant.)

**447**   **Shiatsu quick-fix** "Connection shiatsu" can deepen the short, shallow breathing caused by stress. Lie on the floor on your back and place the palm of your right hand on your abdomen, and your left palm on your chest. Hold this position for one minute.

The exercise stimulates the flow of *chi* between your lungs and your kidneys (the "seat" of anxiety), enabling you to relax a little and breathe more deeply.

**448** **Freewheeling** As a contrast to these Eastern-inspired exercises, do some good old-fashioned Western cycling—the perfectly self-sufficient way to travel considerable distances at considerable speed. There's a Zen aspect to the fusion of rider and steed to make a single, aided organism: you are both motor and passenger. Equip your bicycle with a basket so you'll be truly self-contained.

**449** **In the swim** Swimming is an ideal choice of exercise, as it improves fitness without putting undue strain on the joints. Next time you swim, aim to slow down your breathing, and make your movements as rhythmic and effortless as possible. This can bring you a significant degree of inner calm, and there's a bonus in the novelty of inhabiting a different element.

**450 Body's wisdom** "The body is a big sagacity, a plurality with one sense, a war and a peace, a flock, and a shepherd."
FRIEDRICH NIETZSCHE (1844–1900), GERMANY

**451 Mountain high** When you climb to a high peak, you may think that the only way forward is down. But you're more than flesh, bone, and muscle. Imagine you're here to let your spirit off its bodily leash. Scan the distant views. You're a citizen of vast spaces: enjoy your privileges to the full.

**452 Know your limits** Whichever sport you choose to enjoy, make sure you research it well, so that you're aware of its benefits, but also its risks and any necessary precautions. Treat your body with the respect it deserves as the vehicle of your awareness.

[175]

# INNER CALM

**453**    **Quiet please!** Imagine you're looking for a rare bird in the rainforest. Crashing through the undergrowth, you make a great racket. Result: you scare the creature away! Charging headllong through life, without stopping for silent thought, is one way to ensure that the object of your quest will elude you.

**454**    **Subtle sounds** Sit in the quietest room of your home and close your eyes. Listen first to your breathing, then the beating of your heart. Expand your awareness to the quiet sounds within the room, then those you can hear outside. Just listening, to the life inside and around you, can bring balm to the distracted soul.

**455**    **Open ears** "Listen, or your tongue will keep you deaf."
NATIVE AMERICAN PROVERB

**456**    **Dialogue on hold** There's a place for talk, and there's a place for companionable silence. When you're in company, it's good to sit together reflectively at times, within the charmed circle of quiet. Let differences melt away. Sharing silence with someone you love or like is profoundly refreshing.

**457** **The silence of our friends** "In the end, we will remember not the words of our enemies, but the silence of our friends."

MARTIN LUTHER KING, JR. (1929–1968), USA

**458** **Passage to peace** Quaker meetings are completely silent, unless someone feels moved to express themselves, in speech or in song. Quakers believe that this silence helps them discover the "still, small voice" of their conscience or soul. One morning, hold a ten-minute "silent meeting" with yourself. Tune intuitively into your inner wisdom, knowing that if you try to put this into words, you'll gain only a pale approximation of the truth. Let these deeply-felt insights inspire you for the rest of the day.

**459** **Always there** Imagine the silence you hear after listening to a beautiful piece of music, or even just a beautiful chord. Does it have different qualities compared to regular silence? Remember that this quality of silence holding the memory of beauty is always present, even if you can't detect it. Heavenly music lies latent in silence as Michelangelo's statue of David once lay hidden within a lump of marble.

**460**   **Footsteps** "You can hear the footsteps of God when silence reigns in the mind."
SRI SATHYA SAI BABA (BORN 1926), INDIA

**461**   **Mind cave** To find refuge fast, close your eyes and focus on the dark space in front of them. In Sanskrit, this is called the *citta kash*: the "cave of the mind." Stay in this quiet space for a minute or so, with only your breath as companion. Cover your eyes with the palms of your hands and imagine the darkness becoming absolute, grain by grain, until you're looking into pure emptiness: a complete absence of light and form.

**462**   **A difficult art** "The learning of the grammar of silence is an art much more difficult to learn than the grammar of sounds."
IVAN ILLICH (1926–2002), AUSTRIA/USA

**463**   **Eye of the storm** When life is hectic or stressed, remember that every hurricane has its "eye," the still point in the middle of the raging winds. You too can retain a calm center, by remembering that your essential self is immune to circumstances. Trust in your ability to respond to any situation with the courage and wisdom you can draw from the core of your being.

**464    Personal pilgrimage** When you need to reconnect with yourself, take a journey to somewhere rich in meaning for you—a place in nature, a historic building (perhaps one with spiritual overtones), or a viewpoint over land or sea. Think of the journey as a meditation. On arrival, settle down to at least twenty minutes of quiet reflection, drawing energy from the depths of your being and from the atmosphere of the place itself.

# MEDITATION

**465** **Priority** "The affairs of the world will go on forever. Do not delay the practice of meditation."

JETSUN MILAREPA (c.1052–c.1135), TIBET

**466** **Watchfulness** One basic form of meditation involves becoming aware of the mental chatter in your mind. Sit quietly, eyes closed, and notice each thought as it arises. Remain independent of each thought, and don't react. Simply let it go: allow it to drift out of your consciousness, just as it drifted in. Meditate like this for five to ten minutes: the benefits will be subtle but significant.

**467** **Blue sky view** This is a more visual approach to the previous meditation. Imagine your mind as a clear blue sky, and each thought as a passing cloud. Simply let each thought-cloud drift across your view, without your judging or otherwise positively engaging with it. Just observe—again, for five to ten minutes.

**468** **Gaze at a flame** Meditating on a candle, known as *trataka* in yoga, gives the mind a precise point of focus. Light a candle and place it safely in front of you, at eye level. Focus steadily on the flame, blinking as little as possible. Try to empty your mind of everything except the flame. If your mind wanders, gently bring your attention back to its object.

**469** **Labyrinth of truth** Inwardly rehearse your search for awareness with this visualization. Imagine yourself at the entrance to a labyrinth, deciding which way to go. With every turn you take, think of a delusion falling from you. As you walk, you see only the labyrinth walls—yet there's a pattern, as yet unseen. Once you reach the heart of the maze, you suddenly perceive this pattern from above, in a flash of recognition.

**470** **Light touch** Buddhists and yogis often use hand gestures, or *mudras*, during meditation. Try the *dhyana mudra*, the gesture of concentration, said to be similar to the gesture the Buddha himself used in meditation. Sit comfortably and place both hands in your lap with palms facing up, the right palm on top of the left. Allow the tips of your thumbs to touch and push almost imperceptibly against each other: this touch symbolizes the subtle but constant focus needed in meditation.

**471** **Cup of abundance** To invite inspiration and energy into your life, meditate with the mudra known as *pushpaputa*. Place your hands on your thighs, palms up, and form them into a loose cup shape (*above*). Imagine that rosy-pink petals of inspiration are fluttering down from the sky, filling your hands. Quietly repeat the Zen proverb: "Be as a cup and the universe flows into you."

**472** **Open your heart** Enhance your ability to act from the heart by practicing the Lotus Mudra. Hold your hands together in the center of your chest, with the heels of your palms, pinkies, and thumbs touching. Spread out your other fingers like blossoming petals. As you breathe in, bring your fingertips together, like a bud. As you breathe out, slowly open them again, imagining your heart opening in the same way. Repeat five to ten times.

**473** **Vital breath** Focusing on the breath is one of the most effective ways to awareness, said to be a favorite method of the Buddha. Sit comfortably and close your eyes. Breathe normally and notice how far the air travels. Now draw your breath deeper into your lungs and breathe slowly and evenly. Concentrate on breathing in this way for a few minutes. Notice how each breath arises, departs, and is followed by another. Reflect on how this cycle mirrors the eternal rhythm of life, death, and rebirth.

**474** **The natural pause** At the end of every exhalation and inhalation, your body experiences a natural pause called an *apnea*, from the Greek words *a* (without) and *pnein* (breathing). This is a state of bodily equilibrium, when all your breathing structures relax. Bring your attention to your breathing, and detect these natural pauses. Can you elongate them, without straining your breath? There's a distinct quality of peaceful awareness to these pauses. See if you can find this stillness, and leave your mind there as you continue breathing normally.

**475**   **Bee breath** *Bhramari* (humming bee) breathing recreates the deep, steady sound of a bee in flight. Sit comfortably with your spine erect, hands resting on your knees. Inhale deeply through both nostrils. As you exhale, hum gently until your lungs have emptied. Keep your jaw and neck relaxed throughout. Repeat three to five times: try humming at different pitches, observing the effects on your energy levels.

**476**   **Om** The Vedic mantra "Om" (pronounced *a-u-m*) is said to be the primal sound from which the universe was created. Chanting "Om" tunes you in to this sacred energy. Sit quietly, eyes closed. Chant the first syllable, making the sound last as long as possible; let it resonate around and through you. Then chant the other (two) syllables in turn. Finally, join the syllables into one sound. Repeat rhythmically until your chanting becomes effortless.

**477**  **Om shanti shanti shanti** This Hindu mantra is a prayer for peace—*shanti* means "peace" in Sanskrit. Whenever you find yourself in need of calm and clarity, try using this mantra. Enunciate each syllable mindfully, making the "a" sound long.

**478**  **Sparkling pure** The Buddhist mantra "Om mane padme hum" translates as "Hail to the jewel in the lotus," and is associated with the *bodhisattva* of compassion, Avalokiteshvara, who vowed to help all suffering beings. It's said that if someone recites the mantra 1,000 times a day, the list of benefits that will follow is never-ending. Recite the mantra just ten or twenty times, and notice if you gain peace and clarity.

**479**  **Breath mantra** Yogis believe that the unconscious sound of the in-breath is "so," while that of the out-breath is "hum." Together, these Sanskrit terms mean "He am I" and "We are one"—a constant reminder of our oneness with the divine, and everyone and everything around us. If you feel disconnected, or lonely, recite this mantra.

**480**    **Careful steps** Next time you're in a park or on a beach, practice *kinhin* (walking meditation). Walk slowly and deliberately, bringing complete attention to the placement of your feet—heel, ball of foot, toe—and how you transfer your weight on each step. Adopt the traditional hand gesture if you wish: make your right hand into a fist (thumb inside) and grasp this fist with your other hand. *Kinhin* is a Zen technique—simple yet effective.

**481**    **No books** "Meditation ... may think down hours to moments. Here the heart may give a useful lesson to the head and learning wiser grow without his books."
WILLIAM COWPER (1731–1800), ENGLAND

**482**    **Sit still** *Vipassana* meditation involves sitting absolutely still for long periods. Set an alarm to go off in thirty minutes, and settle into position. Sit on the floor with your back straight, if you can; otherwise, sit on a chair. Close your eyes and be still. Focus on your breath's passage in your nostrils. Observe what happens in your mind and body when you override any desire to move. The practice develops profound awareness and, eventually, insight.

**483**    **Moonstruck** The moon offers an appealing focus for a visual meditation if you can contrive to obtain a decent view. Before you begin, think about the moon's coolness and serenity. While meditating, allow your mind to be filled with the image of the moon and an appeciation of its qualities. Any clouds drifting over the satellite add an atmospheric bonus.

**484**    **Five states** According to yoga, the meditating mind has five forms: the first is complete agitation (*ksiptam*), while the fifth, highest state is complete stillness and stability (*nirodha*). The intervening stages are dullness (*mudha*), brief focus (*viksiptam*), and one-pointedness (*ekagrata*). Even experienced meditators describe their practice as mostly moving between *viksiptam* and *ekagrata*, with occasional glimpses of *nirodha*. Be comforted by this thought as you move toward your own form of stillness.

**485** **Palace of the gods** Mandalas are symbolic images of the cosmos, usually composed of geometric forms, including concentric squares and/or circles. In Hindu and Buddhist traditions they are used as aids to meditation. Focus on a fixed point, at or just above the center of the mandala. Keep your mind as still as possible as you meditate, letting the image sit in your consciousness. One day, looking back on your meditation, you may feel a sense of "cosmic consciousness"—a sense that you are an integral part of the cosmos, which in turn is contained, paradoxically, within your infinite mind.

**486** **Rug lore** If you have an oriental rug, use it as a mandala for meditation. Most such rugs include symbolism of color, number, and shape. In the center is often a dot, symbolizing God, or Mecca. Yellow denotes abundance; blue, the mystic sky; green, spring growth and paradise. Discover the emblematic meanings of your own particular rug and build them into your practice.

**487** **Helpmate** Sit with your eyes closed and visualize a spiritual figure whom you revere, such as Jesus or the Buddha, sitting

opposite you. Imagine them radiating love and wisdom, in a brilliant white light that forms an arc and flows in through the top of your head, down into your heart, bringing with it the love and wisdom of this great healer.

**488**    **Dawn and dusk** "We should meditate upon the Lord daily, especially at dawn and dusk, when the atmosphere is peaceful. Meditation improves faith, devotion, and self-confidence."
THE SAMAVEDA (c.1st CENTURY BCE), INDIA

## WAYS OF THINKING

**489**    **Lost bearings** We speak of "losing ourselves" in profound and absorbing experiences, and the metaphor is an apt one. Take this idea literally and visit somewhere completely new to you—a stretch of countryside, a safe area of a city. Use a map to plan a walk, and set off with refreshments. At a certain point, tuck the map away and walk from memory. When you become disorientated, relish this liberating sensation. Appreciate what you discover. In unfamiliar territory we can learn how to see again.

**490**    **Inward, outward** Awareness that focuses entirely inward, into the mind, the spirit, and the self, while failing to give due attention to the wonders of nature and the universe, is merely a partial experience. To travel onward we need to go joyfully out into the world as well as deep into the recesses of our being.

**491**    **Wishes and goals** A key principle of awareness is that we can't rely on the process of cause and effect, nor on other people to act according to our wishes—so we must relinquish those wishes. To work at controlling the uncontrollable, or to wish for the impossible, wastes energy better spent on achievable goals.

**492**    **Chain reaction** "When you do not accept what actually is, where does that leave you? You need then something else to take its place. The faculty of producing something else is what we call the mind. And then a long chain starts—a series of actions and reactions, being and not being, good and evil, death and suffering. All these come into being as links of that chain. How are they produced? By denial. By denying what is. By negating it. By creating something else in its place."

SWAMI PRAJNANPAD (1891–1974), INDIA

**493**    **Aware now** There's a famous Zen saying: "If not now, when?" This is a pithy way of reminding us that nothing can exist outside the moment. By living in the now, you deprive pointless anxiety and other destructive emotions of their oxygen. The self becomes wholly alive in its element. Awareness is the full appreciation of the self's relationship with now.

**494**    **Positive thinking** See the world in terms of the possibilities it offers rather than the limitations it imposes. Limits are often illusory: they are there because of over-modest expectations.

**495**     **Inner smile** Imagine you're smiling, without moving your lips. In China a similar approach is said to activate *tan tien*, the energy store just below the navel. Allow the smile to travel within you and sit in your abdomen, radiating warmth through your being.

**496**     **Out loud** Use affirmations to assert your ideals. Speak as if you've already attained the state of mind to which you aspire— for example, "I am at peace" or "I am an endless fountain of loving energy." Affirmations like this dissolve time, the future tense of intention, which can be a barrier to new states of being.

**497**     **Half-truths** Cognitive behavioral therapy (CBT) holds that what we perceive to be true about our lives may be partly—or completely—false. Distress or unhappiness can trap us in a vicious circle: we feel bad about ourselves, which gives us a negative view of our predicament, which makes us feel worse. CBT disrupts this cycle, by breaking down sequences of events to view each event individually, preventing future thoughts or actions from being based on negative assumptions. Try this approach. Reconsider some negative assumptions about your life.

**498**   **Good labels** Describing to yourself the character of your own thoughts, and even attaching a simplistic, self-deprecating label to them, can help you to avoid taking yourself too seriously. Try labeling thoughts "useful" or "non-useful"; or perhaps "worry," "to do," and "memory." Notice if doing this helps you gain a sense of detachment.

**499**   **Clear air** Every time you reject a weak or negative thought because it's unworthy of you, you create space for something better. This process operates like breathing—fresh air flows in automatically to replace the stale air you breathe out. There can be no life where there's no breath: apply this logic to your inner life too, and feel yourself thoroughly refreshed.

**500**   **Who am I?** When you're watching your thoughts during meditation, ask yourself, "Am I still there between thoughts?" and "Who is this watching me?" Such searching questions may lead to the ultimate existential question, "Who am I?" One day, when you're ready, the answer will no doubt present itself from deep within your unconscious mind.

**501** **Mysteries** In the Chinese tradition, topographical features are believed to have their own energy—which in turn can affect ours. Recognizing such affinities can help us know where we want to be, which is a good foundation for contentment. Nothing is quite what it seems. Look for the energies beneath the surface, the hidden potential, the secret springs, the mysteries that cloak themselves in the familiar.

**502** **Travelers** "We are not human beings on a spiritual journey, we are spiritual beings on a human journey."
NATIVE AMERICAN SAYING

**503** **Teacher within** Hindus believe that we all have an inner guru or teacher—our higher consciousness, which is said to reside in the third eye, or *ajna chakra*, the subtle energy center located between your eyebrows. When you need a new perspective on a decision or situation, sit comfortably, close your eyes, and bring your middle and index fingertips to the space just above and between your eyebrows. Connect to your inner guru.

**504** **Like a lotus** According to Tantric philosophy, contemplation of the lotus aids spiritual growth. Visualize yourself as a beautiful lotus flower, emerging from the mud of materialism, through the waters of experience toward the sunshine of enlightenment, where you blossom. Just as the lotus stands in the mud and the water, but has its own transcendent substance, so the events and circumstance of your life surround you, but are not part of your unique essence: so you need not identify yourself with them. Grow always toward the light.

**505** **Nature in ourselves** "Nature is often hidden; sometimes overcome; seldom extinguished."
FRANCIS BACON (1561–1626), ENGLAND

**506** **Be lighter** Emotional attachments, which often involve both yearning and nostalgia, deaden our appreciation of the now. To yearn is to inhabit an imagined dream space; to be nostalgic is to inhabit a rose-tinted memory of past times. Neither of these is a desirable residence for the waking soul. Move to a new neighborhood: the evolving present.

**507** **Filter** "You cannot perceive beauty but with a serene mind."
HENRY DAVID THOREAU (1817–1862), USA

**508** **Shades of contentment** Make a distinction between
happiness, which is an emotion, and joy, which is a state of
being. Happiness is precarious—it depends on health, good
fortune, and the satisfaction of various conditions (even the
weather if you're planning a picnic). Joy is the positive energy
that arises from awareness. It's the default setting of the balanced
soul. Nothing can take joy away from you once you find it within.

## PROFOUND ENERGIES

**509**     **Affinities** According to the "law of attraction," if we focus on what we want, and believe truly that it's possible and that we deserve it, that person, object, or situation will move toward us. But if we focus on a feared outcome, that will arrive instead. Watch for the signs—the telltale clues that destiny gives about the future it has in mind for us. Act on them promptly.

**510**     **Channeling the flow** By borrowing the Chinese art of feng shui, we can ensure that every aspect of the home encourages a healthy flow of *chi*, or vital energy. Experiment with a few feng shui principles. For calmness, minimize clutter and maximize space around your furniture; to revitalize social areas, use the color red on walls; to invite healthy energy into your home, keep shoes away from the front door; to keep the *chi* flowing in dark areas, point mirrors toward them.

**511**     **Birthstones** Buy your birthstone for yourself—or perhaps a piece of jewelry incorporating it: garnet (January), amethyst (February), aquamarine (March), diamond (April), emerald (May), moonstone (June), ruby (July), peridot (August), sapphire

(September), opal (October), topaz (November), turquoise (December). Wear or carry this jewel with you to access your inner resources. Touch the stone and imagine its energizing power coursing through your fingers and traveling deep into the heart of your being.

**512** **Tarot talk** The Tarot is a powerful tool for psychological self-examination—to use it for simple fortune-telling trivializes an important tradition. Explore the depths of your psyche by means of such cards as the Hanged Man, the Moon, the Fool, and the Lovers. But let the future take care of itself, under the approximate guidance of your own decisions and actions.

**513** **What we wear** Devotees of the Kabbalah often wear a red string around their left wrist as a spiritual vaccine against evil and negativity (on the grounds that energy is absorbed through the left side of the body). Invest in an item of clothing or jewelry with empowering or protective qualities, and see what happens. Talismans have power by virtue of their chosen symbolism, and can help to focus the mind.

# ONENESS

**514**  **Figure in a landscape** Chinese landscape paintings often include tiny figures—as if to emphasize the grandeur of nature, of which humankind is one small part. Think of the world in these terms, as larger in scale than the human. This is a healthy corrective to the commonplace view that people own the land, which exists to serve their purposes. Think big and live small.

**515**  **Blades of grass** When we think of "places," we think big. But an area of just a few square yards can be described as a place—a patch of a wood or of a public park. Find one of these small-scale places and get to know it thoroughly. Narrow your focus and look closely. There might be interesting insects or invertebrates, or a fascinating fragment of litter. If there's nothing else, just look at the blades of grass—Walt Whitman wrote a great work of poetry on the subject (see pages 295–6), so why should you not find something inspiring in this humble phenomenon of nature?

**516**  **Slow but steady** "Nature does not hurry, yet everything is accomplished."

LAO TZU (c.604–c.531BCE), CHINA

**517** **Microcosms** Fractals are particular shapes that
are found in mathematics and certain natural
organisms, repeated over and over at increasingly
smaller scales. Find an example of a fractal—for example,
a computer-generated diagram, or a natural form such as a
snowflake or a fern. Contemplate how the tiniest part of the
pattern is a minute expression of the whole. Perhaps there is
an element of this in our spirit's relationship with the divine?

**518** **All things and I** "Heaven and Earth and I live together, and
all things and I are one."
CHUANG TZU (c.4TH CENTURY BCE), CHINA

**519** **Star of David** The six-pointed Star of David comprises two
interlocking equilateral triangles, symbols of the male and female
principles, which combine to form the universe. Draw this figure
on a sheet of paper, using double lines for the triangles' sides
(as if they were solid). Each side must in turn go under and over
the sides it encounters. Meditate on the resulting star. Let the
energies of its harmony be absorbed into your spirit.

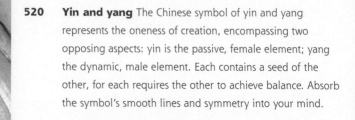

**520** **Yin and yang** The Chinese symbol of yin and yang represents the oneness of creation, encompassing two opposing aspects: yin is the passive, female element; yang the dynamic, male element. Each contains a seed of the other, for each requires the other to achieve balance. Absorb the symbol's smooth lines and symmetry into your mind.

**521** **Masculine feminine** When meeting a stranger, the first thing we register is their gender. Try thinking for a while of men as "she" and "her" and women as "he" and "him." Imagine that every man has a largely female inner self to balance his masculine outer self, and every woman, similarly, a largely male inner self. Consider how the world might be a better place if this were the norm.

**522** **Shell sign** Christian pilgrims of old had as their symbol the scallop shell. Appropriately, the shell resembles the female organs: whatever your gender, you'll need to be receptive, and release your feminine side, to let wisdom dawn. Adopt it as your own personal talisman on your journey to awareness.

**523** **Transcendence** Vedanta is "the end of knowledge," one of the six viewpoints (*darsanas*) of Hindu philosophy. The goal of a spiritual seeker, according to this idea, is to transcend self-identity. We reach self-realization through understanding that there's no separation between the self and the divine (Brahman). The Upanishads provide this philosophy with some of its key texts—read some selections, and open yourself to Oneness.

**524** **Advaita** One school of Vedanta (see **523**), Advaita Vedanta, believes that the world is an illusion (*maya*) created by Brahman. Realizing that we are our own immortal souls (*jivatman*) and that these are not separate from Brahman, we tear down the veil of illusion and are liberated. It's impossible to achieve this change through intellect and reason alone: *advaita* is a state of transcendence that arises through deep understanding (*jnana*). Ponder the lessons of this tradition in your spiritual quest.

**525** **Not so fast** Advaita literally means non-dualism (*a-dvaita*). The yoga teacher T.K.V. Desikachar wrote that even the word implies the existence of dualism, so we have to recognize duality before we can move toward non-duality. Consider everyday dualities—hot and cold, for example, or night and day. Can you see how they share each other's essence? Relax your discriminating mind, and see if you can apprehend harmony.

**526** **Pass beyond** "When we have passed beyond knowing, then we shall have Knowledge. Reason was the helper; Reason is the bar."
SRI AUROBINDO (1872–1950), INDIA

**527** **Partial view** In some Far Eastern regions a lunar eclipse was believed to be caused by a dragon swallowing the moon. Our understanding is always colored by the culture we inhabit. Even today's Western science is an approximation: on its own terms, it leaves much unexplained. True reality lies beyond understanding. True awareness knows reality directly, as a mystic knows God.

**528** **One world** "For the awakened there is only one world, and they all share it. Those who are asleep live each in their own world ..."
HERACLITUS (c.540–c.480BCE), GREECE

# 5

## MINDFUL DAYS

From dawn to dusk  208
The working day  220
Day's end  226
Living well  232
Leisure time  238
Seasons  244

# FROM DAWN TO DUSK

**529**    **One change** Routine can bring a comforting stability and structure to your day, yet it's new experiences that make us feel we're truly alive. Make a promise to yourself to vary one small part of your routine each day: walk a different route to work, shower in the evening instead of the morning, or vice versa, or buy a different newspaper. Feel the invigorating power of change.

**530**    **Reasoning** "The less routine, the more life."
AMOS BRONSON ALCOTT (1799–1888), USA

**531**    **Breezy start** Begin each day in the expectation that some time, before day's end, you'll receive some good news.

**532**    **Lucky you** Think of the chores you face in the day ahead as a privilege, not a burden. Resolve to enjoy the satisfaction of doing them to the best of your ability. Take pleasure in your skills.

**533**    **Spyhole** "Giving thanks for the moment is the only way to glimpse eternity."
MODERN MEDITATION FROM SEVILLE, SPAIN

**534**    **Santé!** We tend to really appreciate normal health only when we're sick. Resolve, next time you wake up, to notice and celebrate the inestimable value of your health, and the benefits it will bring to the day ahead.

**535**    **Reassess** Take a moment of quiet each morning to check that the plans you made the day before still make sense in the clear morning light. Adjust them as necessary. Embrace fluidity.

**536**    **Thirty minutes** Waking up to a beautiful day naturally lifts our spirits, but scientists at the University of Michigan have found that in order to fully benefit from the mood-enhancing properties of good weather, we need to spend at least thirty minutes outside—a tall order if you've a busy day ahead. Next time the sun is shining, plan a half-hour of appreciation: take your lunch to the park, or include walking time in your journey to work.

**537**    **On beauty** "Never lose an opportunity of seeing anything beautiful, for beauty is God's handwriting."
RALPH WALDO EMERSON (1803–1882), USA

**538** **Early riser** Plan to rise one hour earlier for a week. Consider your extra hour a personal bonus, and use it for the things you usually don't have time for: meditation, or yoga, or taking a walk and noticing how different everything appears before the day's routines have taken hold.

At least once a month, **watch the sunrise (539)**, a refreshing experience for mind and spirit, especially at the start of new life phases.

**540** **Natural rhythms** On the weekends, turn off your alarm clock and allow the sun's light

and warmth to gently wake you. This will restore your body's circadian rhythms, maximizing your concentration.

**541** **Work ahead** "Awake, my soul, and with the sun
Thy daily stage of duty run."
THOMAS KEN (1637–1711), ENGLAND

**542** **Empty-headed** On cold winter mornings, ignore the mind's siren song: "Too tired, too cold, too early ..." Don't start thinking about getting up, or running through what the day holds. Keep your mind quiet, channel all your energy into throwing off the covers, and jump thoughtlessly into your day!

**543** **Special theme** Set an intention for your day, such as "Today I will be a good listener" or "Today I will not get distracted." Repeat your intention to yourself whenever you tire or lack motivation. Alternatively, set a theme for the day: for example, you might decide you're going to dedicate a day to adventure, or fluidity, or friendship, or inner wealth. All manner of fresh insights will follow.

**544** **Color me happy** The seven colors of the spectrum are said to to have subconscious emotional associations. Apply some of the principles of color therapy when you're dressing in the morning. If it's a gray winter morning, lift your mood with yellow; if you know you'll need sharp reactions for an important meeting, try red; or if you need to radiate calm and be especially articulate, wear something blue.

**545** **Bright and juicy** "Color is the fruit of life."
GUILLAUME APOLLINAIRE (1880–1918), ITALY/FRANCE

**546** **Quiet time** Don't allow TV or computers into your morning routine. Sit still for a while, and look out of your window. Eat your breakfast quietly if you can. Enjoy rare peace, and a sense of potential, before the day's intrusions begin.

**547** **Early blessing** The word *breakfast* refers to "breaking" your night's "fast" with your first meal—fasting has spiritual meaning in many religions. Before you break your fast, give thanks to whatever deity or benign force you choose for this new morning.

**548**   **No skipping** Tempting as it may be
to save time in the morning by missing
the first meal of the day, even a small
snack such as a cereal bar or piece of fruit
will stimulate your metabolism and digestive
system, giving you essential energy for your day.

**549**   **Breakfast stars** Try energy-boosting granola: mix together 4
cups (14 oz/400 g) rolled oats, 1 cup (4 oz/100 g) mixed nuts
and seeds, ¼ cup (2 fl oz/60 ml) maple syrup, 2 tbsp sunflower
oil, and a few drops of vanilla essence. Spread on a baking sheet
and bake at 375°F (190°C/Gas 5) for 20 minutes. Allow to cool
and store in an airtight container. Enjoy your granola with yogurt
or milk, or sprinkle it over a fresh fruit salad.

**550**   **Smooth start** For a delicious breakfast smoothie, blend a small
chopped banana with 6–8 fresh strawberries and 1 cup (9 fl oz/
250 ml) yogurt. For an extra nutritional kick, you could add some
extra frozen berries such as blueberries or raspberries, which are
easy to store in your freezer compartment.

**551**  **Small print** Print out a favorite inspirational text in tiny print and carry it folded up small with your credit and debit cards. Read it whenever you need to be reminded of what you value ... or every time you use a card to make a purchase!

**552**  **A spend-free day** For one day, avoid spending a single cent. Use food you already have. Don't even buy a newspaper—but don't listen to power-consuming TV or radio either: if you want to know the news, ask somebody.

**553**  **Rush hour** If you dread commuting, try changing your routine. Rather than taking the quickest route and means of transport, allow yourself more time, and walk or cycle part of the journey. If there's no option but a long session on public transport, read a book or newspaper, without musical accompaniment: wired music insulates you from life. See if you can work from home one day per week—increasingly feasible nowadays.

**554**  **Driver's affirmation** If you're a regular driver, sit quietly in your car for a few moments before you set off on a journey.

Visualize your loved ones, and affirm to yourself that you'll drive safely and carefully, and be patient with other drivers today.

**555**    **On the road** Stay mindful of your body while you're driving. While you're stationary in traffic, check that you're sitting up as straight as possible. Take your hands off the wheel, flex your fingers, and rotate your wrists. Lift and drop your shoulders a few times, and roll them in circles forward and backward.

**556**    **Stockpile energy** If you feel the need for a snack between breakfast and lunch, choose foods that have a low glycemic index (GI): they'll release their energy slowly, keeping each moment energized. Oatcakes, bananas, nuts, or rye bread are all good options—and they're perfect for emergency snacking if you miss lunch owing to work pressures.

**557**    **Ideal lunch** To ensure your afternoon is as productive as your morning, eat a healthy mix of protein and carbohydrates at lunchtime: for example, a bean-based soup, a salad niçoise, or a chicken sandwich with wholemeal bread. Avoid high-fat options, which will slow your metabolism. Best of all, **pack a lunchbox (558)**: then you can choose the healthiest ingredients yourself.

**559** **Tummy tonic** Practice the yogic Thunderbolt Pose (see page 28) for five minutes after lunch, to enhance digestion: you'll feel lighter and function more effectively.

**560** **Puzzle through** Give your brain a break from monotony at lunchtime: grapple with a cryptic crossword, play chess with a colleague, or solve a sudoku. You'll be mentally refreshed when you return to work.

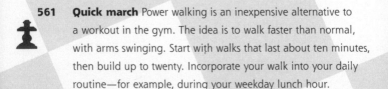

**561** **Quick march** Power walking is an inexpensive alternative to a workout in the gym. The idea is to walk faster than normal, with arms swinging. Start with walks that last about ten minutes, then build up to twenty. Incorporate your walk into your daily routine—for example, during your weekday lunch hour.

**562** **Phone pal** If lunching with friends is impossible, coordinate your breaks for the same time of day, and call each other on the phone. Laughing and catching up with someone you care about will give your day variety, and boost your positive attitude.

**563** **Eye tour** Increase your alertness with toning eye exercises. Without moving your head, look up as far as you can, then down as far as you can, three times. Then look to your right and left, three times. Next, look diagonally up to your right, and down to your left, three times. Finally, diagonally up to your left, followed by diagonally down to your right, three times.

**564** **Healing cup** Black, green, and white teas are delicious, refreshing, and good for us: they contain antioxidants, which protect the body from diseases including cancer. If you prefer herbal infusions, try soothing chamomile, relaxing verbena, stimulating fennel, or tangy peppermint.

**565** **All purpose** "If you are cold, tea will warm you. If you are too heated, it will cool you. If you are depressed, it will cheer you. If you are excited, it will calm you."
WILLIAM GLADSTONE (1809–1898), ENGLAND

**566**  **Tea ceremony** In Japanese culture, the tea ceremony (*chanoyu*, meaning "way of tea") is a detailed ritual, associated with the rigorous discipline of Zen Buddhism. Each stage of the ceremony, from the decoration of the room to the arrival of guests, is carefully planned and has its own symbolism. Central to the ceremony are the tenets of harmony, respect, purity, and tranquility—the ritual of preparing and drinking tea provides a brief sanctuary from the chaos of the outside world. Next time you drink an afternoon cup of tea, savor it. Allow yourself to retreat from the world for a while and feel at peace.

**567**  **A tender accomplishment** "[The tea ceremony] is essentially a worship of the Imperfect, as it is a tender attempt to accomplish something possible in this impossible thing we know as life."
OKAKURA KAKUZŌ (1862–1913), JAPAN

**568**  **Happy hour** "There are few hours in life more agreeable than the hour dedicated to the ceremony known as afternoon tea."
HENRY JAMES (1843–1916), USA/ENGLAND

## THE WORKING DAY

**569**   **For achievement** As you go about your daily business, think of the energy you expend with every action. This energy, as it's processed, polishes the inner trophy of your achieving self. Throw yourself into the bustle of a rich and complex life and aim for a super-shiny finish you can see your face in.

**570**   **Invocation** "Get happiness out of your work or you may never know what happiness is."
ELBERT HUBBARD (1856–1915), USA

**571**   **On time** Cultivate the habit of punctuality. You'll waste less energy worrying about being late, so your morning will be more productive and focused.

When an appointment demands a longish journey, aim to arrive **an hour in advance (572)**—this will completely remove journey stress, and perhaps even give you up to an hour to yourself: take along a book to read or a notebook to scribble in.

**573** **Fresh starts** Take frequent short breaks during your working day. We achieve more at the start and end of periods of work (or learning) than in the middle, so structure your time into disciplined, bite-sized chunks of activity and rest, each with a distinct beginning and ending, and you'll be more productive.

**574** **Each day's work** "Live neither in the past nor in the future, but let each day's work absorb your entire energies, and satisfy your widest ambition."
WILLIAM OSLER (1849–1919), CANADA

**575** **Catlike** The cat stretch is a great way to unwind during the working day. Stand straight and as tall as you can. Loosely roll your shoulders, arms, wrists, and neck, all at the same time. Sit down, ideally on the floor, and rotate your ankles. Clasp your hands around each knee in turn, and bring it toward your chest. You're now ready for another spell of sedentary hard work.

**576** **Quick stretch** If you work in an office, do shoulder stretches from time to time to ease muscular tension. Seated in your chair,

reach out your arms and take a few deep breaths. Lift your right arm above your head and pull your hand, palm down, onto your back. Then stretch your left arm behind you, palm up, and try to bring your two sets of fingertips together until touching. Hold the position for a few seconds, then relax. Repeat on the other side.

**577** **Lunchtime safari** Think of your lunch break as a refreshing mini vacation—an opportunity to connect with your non-working self. Start your break promptly, and try a new type of cuisine for your lunch. Research the cultural landmarks near your workplace, and visit them. Or indulge in a mini beauty treatment.

**578** **Defeat lethargy** Don't underestimate or ignore an afternoon energy slump—you may end up nodding off at your desk. Take action: rehydrate with a glass of cold water, or try some self-massage: rub the palms of your hands together until they are warm, close your eyes, and then circle your palms over your temples. **Review your to-do list (579)** and tackle jobs that involve moving around the office or talking to colleagues, to boost your circulation and alertness.

**580**   **Fire-breathing** When you feel low in confidence, especially before an important meeting, fire yourself up with "dragon's breath." Stand with your feet shoulder-width apart, inhale, and then slowly exhale, making a strong, whispered "haaa" sound. Repeat four times. Each time, imagine you're a dragon, breathing fire: feel empowering energy stirring in your belly.

**581**   **Groundwork** The best rewards are not easily won. If a project seems to be taking forever to come to fruition, imagine yourself as a farmer: preparing the ground, sowing the seeds, caring for them as they grow, and finally harvesting the fruit of your hard labor. Work intensively, involving yourself fully in every stage of your project, and you'll appreciate the results all the more.

**582** **Mind like an arrow** If you're having difficulty concentrating at work, select your most essential task as a target, and imagine your mind like an arrow in flight, one-pointed and unstoppable, completely focused on reaching its goal.

**583** **Permutations** Consider the chess player. Before he makes his move, he must consider every option and multiple possible outcomes. He acts, his opponent responds, and new possibilities present themselves. Approach major decisions and opportunities like a chess player: never looking back unnecessarily, but staying as alert as you can to new potential in your situation.

**584** **Working life** "The harder I work the more I live."
GEORGE BERNARD SHAW (1856–1950), IRELAND/ENGLAND

**585** **Possible dream** The most effective and inspiring workers are those who love their job. If you long to turn a treasured hobby into your profession, don't automatically dismiss this as an idle fantasy. Research training and employment in your area of interest: determination will often produce success.

**586**   **Talents** "Work while you have the light. You are responsible
for the talent that has been entrusted to you."
HENRI FRÉDÉRIC AMIEL (1821–1881), SWITZERLAND

**587**   **Open doors** Take the time to know and remember the home
situations of your closest colleagues and, if appropriate, the
details of their family. Your colleagues will probably return the
gesture. A friendly working environment can be of great value
if your personal life encounters choppy waters.

**588**   **Computer marvel** Modern computer software is incredibly
sophisticated. Show your appreciation to the unknown, ingenious
programmers by taking some time to learn what your software
can really do. It's probably more than you realize, and you're
bound to save time in the future with your new accomplishment.

**589**   **Easy peasy** If you find a task or activity comes naturally to
you, don't allow the end-result to diminish in your own eyes.
Appreciate your skill and ease as a blessing, and honor your
personal acheivements as you would someone else's.

# DAY'S END

**590**    **Evening light** As the sun sets each day, notice the quality of the sky as it moves from afternoon to night. The dusk can be as lovely as the dawn, in its own understated way.

**591**    **Bright star** The planet Venus is sometimes the "morning star," and sometimes the "evening star"—and there are also times when she disappears completely, hidden behind the sun. Locate her in the sky around sunset, not far from the sun itself—she will usually be unmissable, the brightest heavenly body in the sky. Meditate quietly, allowing the planet's purity, clarity, and tranquility to enter your soul.

**592**    **Water worship** To the Celts, water represented a boundary between the physical world and the Otherworld: caves, wells, and springs were regarded as sacred gateways. Consider marking the transition from your working day to your own "otherworld"— your valuable free time—with water. Unwind by taking a relaxing bath or swim, or enjoying a refreshing glass of iced water or maybe a cup of herbal tea.

**593**   **Sleep well** If you're a restless sleeper, try establishing a regular bedtime routine. Follow the same quiet, relaxing pattern in the same order every night before you climb into bed, even if it's as simple as switching off the lights, washing your face, then brushing your teeth. Notice if your sleep improves.

**594**   **Looking back** As you prepare for bed, run through the highlights of the past day and relish the most enjoyable of them. Put aside your uncomfortable memories to learn from tomorrow. Also, take a few minutes to **praise yourself (595)**. Congratulate yourself on the achievements of the day. Assign unfinished tasks to another day (not necessarily tomorrow), in the knowledge that you've done your best.

**596**   **Sleep disk** As you lie in bed, visualize a rainbow-patterned disk nestled near your heart. Imagine it gathering speed in a rapid spin, until all the colors turn white. Hold in your mind this image of the spinning white disk as you drift into the realm of sleep.

[227]

**597**   **Dreamtime** Native Australians believe that the Dreamtime is the creative force that underlies the universe. Recognize the potential value of dreams, and their meanings, in your own life, and read up on dream pioneers, such as Carl Jung, Sigmund Freud, and Fritz Perls. You'll be able to interpret your dreams, and benefit your self-development, from an informed perspective.

**598**   **Night journal** Keep a notebook by your bed so that you can note down your dreams. Observe any images and themes that recur. Emerging patterns will bring clear answers to the question of what, deep down, are the issues that are preoccupying you.

**599**   **In your dreams** Be aware of common dream symbolism: for example, animals represent our instinctual drives and desires; water symbolizes our unconscious; and buildings connect to our feelings about ourselves and our bodies.

**600** **Deep down** "Dreams are the touchstones of our characters."
HENRY DAVID THOREAU (1817–1862), USA

**601** **Book at bedtime** Many find that reading eases their transition into a good night's sleep. Experiment with different content, and its effect on your sleep. It may be wise to choose a book for its atmosphere, and leave intellectual content for the daytime.

**602** **Silent night** We often underestimate the power of rest to rejuvenate both our bodies and our minds. Recognize a good night's sleep for the treasure that it is, and make quality rest and relaxation priorities in your life. Be tough on sleep thieves!

**603** **Fail-safe** "A good laugh and a long sleep are the best cures in the doctor's book."
IRISH PROVERB

**604** **Sanctuary** In feng shui, the bedroom is known as "the snake's nest": the snake is a symbol of health and energy. Feng shui guidelines for the bedroom include using rich colors for bed linen (they'll enclose you in a stable energy field while you sleep) and keeping plants out of the bedroom, since their energy is too stimulating. The area around your bed should be dedicated to inactivity, so keep TV and laptops in another room ... and never, ever be tempted to read work documents in bed!

**605** **Light and dark** Many of us greet total darkness with trepidation, but scientists believe that sleeping in the dark may have benefits for our health—plus, overcoming irrational fears like this can help us be more assertive during the day. Next time you have the opportunity, spend the night in utter darkness.

**606** **Pillow of conscience** Peaceful sleep depends on knowing that you've acted well during the day. Think of the untroubled night to come as your reward for compassion and truthfulness—and a symbol of your commitment to goodness.

**607** **Just reward** "Sleeping is no mean art: for its sake one must stay awake all day."
FRIEDRICH NIETZSCHE (1844–1900), GERMANY

# LIVING WELL

**608**    **Sweet home** Make your home look as welcoming as possible. Keep paintwork fresh, and use pot plants, small shrubs, or climbing plants on trellises if you have space. Friends will delight in visiting, and returning home will be a perennial joy.

**609**    **Feeding the home** In Chinese, the word *kou* means both "mouth" and "front door": the door is the gateway to the home, the mouth is the gateway to the body, and both are responsible for letting *chi* (life energy) into our dwelling place. In feng shui terms, a solid front door, or one with small glass panes, will retain *chi* in the home. However, if you already have a transparent door, fitting a curtain on the inside will serve the same purpose.

**610**    **DIY joy** Equip yourself with some basic home improvement tools: screwdrivers, a wrench, a power drill. Take pleasure in using them for straightforward household tasks such as hanging pictures or rewiring lamps. Don't be discouraged if you try and fail, and don't hesitate to enlist friends or expert help if you need to—you're bound to learn some new basic skills!

**611**    **Happiest man** "He is the happiest, be he king or peasant, who finds peace in his home."

JOHANN WOLFGANG VON GOETHE (1749–1832), GERMANY

**612**    **Tidy home, tidy mind** When it comes to the hidden interior spaces of your home such as drawers and cupboards, don't allow cynicism to creep in—"if we can't see it, it doesn't matter." Be as house-proud of the invisible spaces as the visible ones, and enjoy feeling serenely organized.

**613**    **Refined dining** In feng shui, the dining area is viewed as the
the center of wealth, both financial and spiritual. Invest some
time and energy into this space: create a calming mood with
plain colors and simple shapes, and encourage the smooth
flow of energy (*chi*) with curved objects and surfaces.

**614**    **Eat less meat** It's healthier, will make you feel better, and
contributes to solving one of the biggest problems facing the
planet: the fact that animals compete with humans for vital
foodstocks. Explore alternative sources of protein.

**615**    **Vital veg** Get into the habit of eating plenty of fresh fruit and
vegetables every day. They contribute to our well-being by
boosting the immune system, while at the same time providing
us with a living connection with the vital energy of the earth.

**616**    **Fibertastic** It's a daily challenge to eat enough dietary fiber—
the typical US citizen eats just 11 g per day, although experts
recommend 18–20 g. Fiber is present only in plant foods, so try
replacing the meat in one evening meal per week with beans

or pulses, or snacking on fruit and fresh vegetables. You'll soon see lasting benefits for your digestive health, helping you to live more energetically—and comfortably—in the present moment.

**617**    **Keep moving** Our bodies are made to move—any activity in which we remain mostly static for long periods, including sitting or standing, will make us stiff and uncomfortable. Balance your different types of activity: still and moving, mental and physical. Keeping active will help you to function as a rounded person.

**618**    **Step by step** Health experts recommend we walk 10,000 steps per day. Buy a pedometer: see how often you can hit this target.

**619**    **Summer bounty** During the summer, make a special effort to eat seasonal fruit for breakfast: for example, strawberries, raspberries, peaches, or apricots. Enjoy their succulence and fragrance, epitomizing the season.

**620**    **Fruit juice plus** Freshly squeezed fruit and vegetable juices are revitalizing and delicious: they contain little fiber, but their nutrients are speedily absorbed. Try mixing vegetables with fruits as part of your juicing routine. Carrot and orange is a classic combination; or try apple and beet, or celery and pomegranate.

**621** **Superfood** Boost your energy with a glass of wheatgrass juice: it's rich in vitamins, minerals, and enzymes, and even contains amino acids, the building blocks of protein.

**622** **Simple thanks** Saying grace can provide a wonderful moment of thankful meditation before a meal. It need not be religious: simply giving thanks to the animals and plants who have given up their lives to make the meal, and to friends and family for coming together at the table, can be enough.

**623** **Refreshment** "May this food restore our strength, giving new energy to tired limbs, new thoughts to weary minds. May this drink restore our souls, giving new vision to dry spirits, new warmth to cold hearts."
TRADITIONAL IRISH GRACE

**624    Thinking of others** "All living beings suffer in this life. May they all have enough food to eat today."
BUDDHIST BLESSING, TRADITIONALLY SAID BEFORE A MEAL

**625    Explore flavor** Most of us should eat less salt—yet food without it can seem bland and tasteless. Next time you're cooking a dish from scratch, skip the salt, and experiment instead with piquant chili, refreshing citrus, or heartening herbs. Savor the new ingredients, and ask yourself if you truly miss the salt.

# LEISURE TIME

**626**    **Downtime** Ensure you have at least two hours of uninterrupted leisure each week. Use these hours however you choose, but always find time to really relax. Your refreshed outlook will benefit every area of your life.

**627**    **Pet projects** Don't just stick to routine in your spare-time activities: explore opportunities to develop them in new, stimulating directions. If you're part of a book group, organize a trip to a reading by your favorite author. Or work toward a charity concert with your singing group. If you're a runner, look into training for a half-marathon.

**628**    **Self-practice** If you take a weekly exercise class, ask your teacher to write down for you some exercises, and provide guidance in home practice. Your body is like an instrument, and will perform better the more you cherish it. This way, also, you'll be adding value to your regular class.

**629**    **Illuminate a blind spot** Use your leisure time to delve into a new area of knowledge or learn a new skill that you've always felt drawn to. If you love music, buy a book on musical theory and master the rudiments. If you wish you hadn't dropped math or languages in your youth, relearn some basics now. If you love art, tour a collection. Flesh out your interests: make them vital.

**630** **Connections** Enter the labyrinth of connected interests: a sailing trip might lead to an interest in seabirds, or a theater outing to a visit to a new gourmet restaurant near by. Rejoice in the eye-opening side-paths of your pastime, and have fun exploring.

**631** **Unlearn dependencies** Master various skills so that you can manage more tasks for yourself—everything from touching up scratches on your car to replacing a broken zipper. Each new skill learned is a source of independence and inspiration, will save you money and time, and give you more opportunities to help your friends and family.

**632** **Melody and meditation** Immerse yourself fully in music whenever you listen. To do this, it's best to play music when you're relaxing, and can give it your undivided attention. Use portable music devices wisely: you'll be unable to surrender yourself to the music if you're engaged in another activity.

**633**   **Whispered secrets** "Music takes us out of the actual and whispers to us dim secrets that startle our wonder as to who we are, and for what, whence, and whereto."
RALPH WALDO EMERSON (1803–1882), USA

**634**   **The greats** Don't be intimidated by genius—the Beethovens, the Tolstoys, the Picassos. Immerse yourself in their worlds. Admire and be transformed.

**635**   **The Muses' corrective** "Harmony, which has movements akin to the revolutions of our souls … was meant to correct any discord which may have arisen in the courses of the soul, and to be our ally in bringing her into harmony and agreement with herself. Rhythm too was given by the Muses for the same reason, on account of the irregular and clumsy ways which prevail among mankind generally, and to help us against them."
PLATO (c.427–c.347BCE), GREECE

**636** **Local wonders** Take a short vacation to explore the areas of historical interest or outstanding natural beauty near your home. You'll return to work refreshed—but free of travel tiredness!

**637** **True vision** "The voyage of discovery is not in seeking new landscapes but in having new eyes."
MARCEL PROUST (1871–1922), FRANCE

**638** **All aboard** Spend the day on a sailboat. Time spent on the water is naturally refreshing and energizing, and viewing the land from the water can be illuminating. If you're not already familiar with them, learn some of the rudiments of sailing.

**639** **Voyage** "Throw off the bowlines. Sail away from the safe harbor. Catch the trade winds in your sails. Explore. Dream. Discover."
MARK TWAIN (1835–1910), USA

**640** **Active tourist** If you plan to travel abroad on vacation, make an effort to learn a few words of the language before you go. A little knowledge and a few words of dialect will plug you into local culture, and ease connections with local people, making your adventures that little bit more rewarding (and intelligible).

**641** **Certain cure** "Travel is fatal to prejudice, bigotry, and narrow-mindedness …"

MARK TWAIN (1835–1910), USA

**642** **Research** Read a book set in the area you'll be visiting before you go, perhaps by a local author. This could be a novel, or history,

or nature, or politics—whatever most interests you. Try to make connections between what you read and what you see or hear.

**643** **Obligatory** "Every man who possibly can should force himself to a holiday of a full month in a year, whether he feels like it or not." WILLIAM JAMES (1842–1910), USA

**644** **Out of control** If your travel plans go awry and things turn out differently than you expected, view the resultant changes as all part of the adventure. As John Steinbeck said, "The certain way to be wrong [about a journey] is to think you control it."

**645** **Diverse dishes** Be brave—sample some regional dishes while you're abroad, no matter how unfamiliar the ingredients may seem. They'll often be fresh, seasonal, and prepared with pride— and they may even have hidden health benefits.

**646** **Finding new vigor** "Travel and change of place impart new vigor to the mind." SENECA (c.4BCE–65CE), ROME

## SEASONS

**647** **Blossom viewing** In springtime, follow the custom of the Japanese and search out the buds and blossom of flowering trees. In Japan, the brief, sublimely beautiful emergence of the cherry blossom (*sakura*) represents the sweetness and transience of life itself. Respond with your own meditative celebration of new life.

**648** **Seasons change** "Sitting quietly, doing nothing, spring comes, and the grass grows by itself."
BUDDHIST PROVERB

**649** **The turning year** Honor the life-giving power of the sun: stay up all night to watch the sunrise on the longest day (June 21 in the Northern Hemisphere). Celebrate with a great breakfast.

**650** **Two beautiful words** "Summer afternoon—Summer afternoon … the two most beautiful words in the English language."
HENRY JAMES (1843–1916), USA/ENGLAND

**651** **Good and bad weather** Don't hide indoors—appreciate the extremes of inclement weather just as you would a perfect sunny

day. Wrap up warm (or waterproof), and enjoy the freezing air on your face. Splash through rainy puddles. You'll feel exhilarated, and all the more appreciative of your warm, dry home.

652    **Harvest home** Harvesting is a time-honored activity, and one that is easy to participate in during the summer and fall. If you don't have a garden or fruit trees, find a local farm that offers fruit or vegetable picking, and join in. Enjoy the textures, sights, and fragrances of the ripening year.

**653**   **Catch a falling leaf** It's said that each time you catch a fall leaf as it drops from a tree, you win a wish for the coming year. And there are few more hilarious, live-in-the-moment activities than chasing leaves around on a golden autumn afternoon. Catching them is harder than you think, but each time you succeed, close your eyes, and make your wish.

**654**   **Winter warmer** In Chinese medicine, winter is the "yin" time of year, corresponding to coldness, dark, and damp. To ensure balance, introduce warm, comforting "yang" spices to your diet as the days draw in: add grated fresh gingerroot to your tea, or bake cookies full of uplifting cloves, cinnamon, and nutmeg.

**655**   **New Year prayer** Celebrate the New Year with a ceremony of social harmony and thanksgiving. Even if you're not going to a party, venture out into the street, or at least switch on the TV. On the stroke of midnight, make a gesture of peace such as joining hands with everyone—pray for blessings for the year to come.

**656**   **Light and sparkle** Celebrate the New Year as the Chinese do, with firecrackers. The idea, originally, was to scare away evil spirits and bad luck—and to awaken the golden dragon, which would then fly through the sky, bringing rain to the crops. Think of these things as you light the first cracker: after all, the primordial truths are universal, and still have meaning today.

**657**   **Resolution** "Be always at war with your vices, at peace with your neighbors, and let each new year find you a better man." BENJAMIN FRANKLIN (1706–1790), USA

# 6

## LIVING FROM A GOLDEN HEART

Goodness 250

Acceptance and patience 257

Forgiveness 262

Generosity 264

Gratitude 270

Courage 272

Truthfulness 276

Selflessness 279

Detachment 281

Love and compassion 283

Sense of humor 291

# GOODNESS

**658**    **Active ways** We tend to talk of virtues as abstract nouns—truth, forgiveness, courage. But the natural form of any virtue is the verb: we follow the truth, forgive people, act bravely. Inhabit those abstractions and bring them vividly to life.

**659**    **Fruits of action** The principle of karma may be summarized as follows: "Every action brings an appropriate consequence upon the doer." Karma is not prescriptive: it relies on our intuition and our conscience to direct us. In our hearts we usually know how to behave: listen to that inner voice and ensure that you reap a karmic harvest, not a karmic whirlwind.

**660**    **Building blocks** An ethically responsible life is one of the most reliable paths to contentment. One of our most precious gifts is the knowledge that no one would doubt that our behavior is well meant. Thoughtful good intentions, combined with selfless, courageous action, are the cornerstones of a happy life.

**661**   **Under observation** When you're alone—meditating perhaps, or traveling to work—you may have limited opportunities to practice the virtues you believe in. Imagine, at these times, that your every thought and feeling are being monitored on a hypersensitive instrument. Would anything it detected make you feel uncomfortable? If so, this is the area you need to concentrate on in your next session of self-examination.

**662**   **Down the line** Native Americans make decisions with the "seventh generation" in mind—that is, people living seven generations into the future. Take the long view when assessing the consequences of your actions.

**663**  **Who am I?** It's often been said that we become the choices we make. Our identity, in other words, is in large measure developed through the way we behave and act—especially toward other people. Few of us can be saints but we can certainly all be seekers—determined explorers on the path of right thought and right behavior. It is on this path that we will find ourselves.

**664**  **Them and us** To live fully in the present, it helps to assume that people will take responsibility for their own life just as you're taking responsibility for yours. Let them make their own choices. If your values clash, so be it—if you show them acceptance and compassion, perhaps they'll come to see your point of view.

**665**  **Commendable** The principles of the Buddhist Eightfold Path (see page 121) concerned with correct behavior within society are right speech, right action, and right livelihood. To practice *right speech*, resist every impulse to talk negatively about others. Be moderate, considerate, and courteous in what you say ... or resolve to stay quiet if necessary.

**666** **Act wisely** Sincere action is no less important than sincere speech—*right action* means never doing something that would hurt others or yourself. Respect for others, reliability, kindness, and compassion are all key. Living in the moment does not mean acting impulsively, without thought of the future.

**667** **Work well** "The reputation of a thousand years may be determined by the conduct of one hour."
JAPANESE PROVERB

**668** **Good job** *Right livelihood* means making your living in a way that does not cause harm. Your job may be office-based, but an office is not an ivory tower. All jobs have karmic consequences. Weigh these carefully, and try to make a positive impact.

**669** **Conundrums** Nobody said that the good life is easy. Ethics is the branch of philosophy concerned with the complexities and contradictions of moral judgments. You're sure to come across ethical dilemmas, when different imperatives conflict with each other. When this happens, trust your conscience—but don't necessarily expect it to give you a quick answer: it isn't an online search engine!

**670** **Simple living** Spiritual seekers have often extolled the virtues of the simple life, free of superfluous possessions or desires. Consider any areas of your life that feel overcomplicated: can you improve matters by stripping them down to the basics? To simplify is to grow back toward our original innocence.

**671** **Flying high** In Greek mythology Daedalus made artificial wings for his son Icarus, who disobeyed his father by flying too near the sun. The wax of the wings melted, and down tumbled the flyer to his death. This is a parable not against ambition, which is not in itself undesirable, but against arrogance. Temper ambition with humility and it will take you farther.

**672** **Circle of truth** Indian teachings speak of the value of *satsang*, a Sanskrit term meaning "true company." *Satsang* can mean following a guru, but it also can mean spending time with trustworthy people, who nurture and support your onward journey. Seek out such folk in all areas of your life.

**673** **Harmonious** Zen is not just concerned with nature, beauty, and emptiness. At the heart of this distinctive Japanese version of Buddhism is the idea of questioning every aspect and moment of experience in order to realize awareness. In a flash of insight we find truth—enabling us to live in harmony with ourselves and others.

**674** **Keep at it** "There is no failure except in no longer trying."

ELBERT HUBBARD (1856–1915), USA

**675** **Daily renewal** When asked how she manages to run her daily five miles, Oprah Winfrey is reported to have said, "I recommit to it every day of my life." Regularly renew your commitment to goodness—keep your ideals fresh in your mind.

**676** **Model student** The Buddha's son, Rāhula, was an eager and attentive student. Each morning he lifted a handful of sand and said: "May I have today as many words of counsel from my teacher as there are here grains of sand." Follow in Rāhula's footsteps: vow to learn something new from others every day.

**677** **Petal power** Traditionally, the petals of the sacred lotus symbolize our worthiest deeds. Enumerate to yourself the best things you've done over the last year, and for each action you think of, furnish an imaginary lotus with a petal. The result will be an imaginary self-portrait. Gaze on it and affirm your determination to carry on the good work.

# ACCEPTANCE AND PATIENCE

**678**   **Perfect practice** Treat life's challenges as valuable opportunities to practice the combined arts of acceptance and patience. They are as valuable and rewarding as courage and decisiveness.

**679**   **Ignore gnat bites** Life's tiny troubles—like not having a perfect view at the theater, noticing a new scratch on your car, or just missing a train—don't threaten you in any way. Rise above them. Don't dramatize superficial irritations: it makes them more powerful as hazards to your peace of mind.

**680**   **Wisdom of weeds** "A flower falls and fades even though we love it. A weed sprouts up even though we don't love it."
DŌGEN (1200–1253), JAPAN

**681**   **Be content** The teaching of acceptance, or *santosha*, is one of Patanjali's five yogic *niyamas*, or social observances. *Santosha* means contentment, with every aspect of our lives, and with ourselves—from being philosophical if an event doesn't turn out as we expected, to accepting the shape of our bodies. Cultivate this feeling within yourself—life will feel richer.

**682** **Never hungry** "A contented mind is a continual feast."
ENGLISH PROVERB

**683** **Hot and cold** A Buddhist monk asked his master how to avoid extremes of hot and cold. The master advised: "When it's cold, be completely cold; when it's hot, be completely hot." If circumstances are beyond your control, don't invest energy or emotion in them. Ride the reality of the moment. Be empowered by your acceptance.

**684** **Perfect poise** "The ideal individual bears the accidents of life with dignity and grace, making the best of circumstances."
ARISTOTLE (384–322BCE), GREECE

**685** **Cosmos** In the East there's a traditional belief that the world rests on a tortoise's back—which no doubt most Westerners would find bizarre. The beliefs of other cultures may seem self-evidently wrong to you, but in the realm of faith there are few certainties. Freedom of speech and freedom of belief go hand in hand. So whatever you feel about other people's religious or metaphysical views, respect their right to hold them—which doesn't mean, of course, that you need to accept the ways in which fundamentalism (which can be found in any religion) can undermine precious rights and freedoms.

**686**   **Fluid** Be open to different viewpoints, and change your mind if you see new truth in a situation. This is wisdom, not fickleness.

**687**   **Good cheer** If all else fails, ask yourself: Is this something I can laugh about? Of course, some predicaments are too grave for this remedy, but you may be surprised how often your answer is yes.

**688**   **Broadly true** "To live and let live" is a time-honored principle of conduct. There are times when this rule will not apply—when we see someone we love making a mistake, or when we know that someone's behavior is damaging. Yet the dictum remains broadly true. Rely on your intuition to alert you to exceptions.

**689**    **What will be** Railing against fate is unattractive: it imposes a nuisance and a burden upon our friends and family, some of whom might have more reason to complain than we do. On the other hand, to make light of a big problem, or to seem to, tends to be admired. Destiny is deaf to our protestations. So why not make the best of things—with silent patience and fortitude?

**690**    **Them or me?** "The man who makes everything that leads to happiness depend upon himself, and not upon other men, has adopted the very best plan for living happily."
PLATO (c.427–c.347BCE), GREECE

**691**    **Carved in stone** Shakespeare's character Viola, in *Twelfth Night*, describes her sister sitting "like Patience on a monument"—an image of quiet stillness. When you're about to embark on a waiting phase—to discover how a problematic situation turns out, or to see how someone else behaves—remember the Bard's image. Think of yourself as a statue. Stone is not impatient for time to pass: perhaps you can learn from its passivity?

**692** **Changes** It's when life brings changes our way that acceptance is hardest for us. Fresh circumstances often challenge us deeply. In periods of transition, don't rush to make judgments about how comfortable the new situation will be for you. Allow things time to settle down, and face the future with an open mind.

**693** **Wait a while** If you find it hard to empty your mind when you're still and quiet, put yourself into waiting mode—even though you're waiting for nothing specific. Who knows, perhaps some unexpected visitation will occur.

**694** **An ecstatic world** "Stay at your table and listen. You need not even listen, just wait. You need not even wait, just learn to be quiet, still, and solitary. The world will offer itself freely to you, unmasking itself. It has no choice in the matter. It will roll in ecstasy at your feet."

FRANZ KAFKA (1883–1924), CZECH REPUBLIC

# FORGIVENESS

**695**  **Quick and easy** We speak of "bearing" a grudge, and this word
is accurate: resentment is a burden. Forgiveness offers an instant
way to lighten the load of your heart.

**696**  **Move on** If someone apologizes to you, accept their apology
gracefully and without suspicion. Don't be tempted to backtrack
to the point at issue, or to try to make them understand how hurt
or angry you were. If you value the relationship, concentrate on
making it work again. Appreciate the sunshine after the rain—
and put down that umbrella!

**697**  **Forgiving soul** Some people find that forgiveness is one
of the hardest qualities to summon. However, if you live truly
in the present, so that the past simply falls away, forgiveness
ceases to require any effort: it's what's left when resentments
are annihilated by acceptance.

**698**  **Springboard** A sense of betrayal can strike deep in our souls.
Yet life is full of conflicting loyalties and priorities, not to mention
emotions, and perhaps there was inevitably going to be a loser?

Try to understand the bigger picture: with a little imagination and empathy you might see that you've been the victim of circumstances beyond anyone's control. Use this perception as a springboard for your forgiveness.

**699** **What injury?** There's a false kind of virtue, whereby you overtly forgive someone, but privately believe that from now on they remain indebted to you. True forgiveness is absolute and unconditional. It has a short memory.

**700** **In your heart** Don't make a big ritual out of forgiving someone. Otherwise, it will seem as if you wish to be deeply thanked for your magnanimity. It's more a matter of what happens in your heart than a public display of your good character.

**701** **Muddy waters** Often there's no point in continually asking for explanations from people you feel have wounded you. They may be as confused as you are about the chemistry of their motives. In any case, forgiveness does not require a preamble of understanding: it's a gesture of the heart, not of the mind.

# GENEROSITY

**702**    **The giving sun** Benevolence is silent good will, streaming out indiscriminately into the world—into your life. Think of the sun shining in winter, softening the earth, melting the ice: it gives without design or intention to heal. The ground feels no debt to the sun; neither does the sun expect gratitude. Follow the way of benevolence—it's always well lit, even on the darkest night.

**703**    **Shareholders** Find inspiration in the great Indian spiritual leader Mahatma Gandhi, who believed that all our lives are interconnected: if you have wealth in excess of your basic needs, recognize yourself as a trustee, not the owner, of this prosperity. Even the wealth we work hard for is not ours alone: let others receive a generous portion of its dividends.

**704**    **First step** "Whoever desires to be given everything must first give everything away."
MEISTER ECKHART (c.1260–c.1328), GERMANY

**705**    **Meaningful numbers** Celebrate anniversaries with symbolic gifts—offer a friend 21 roses for turning 21, or find an antique silver ornament, in the traditional manner, to mark 25 years of friendship or marriage. After all, every gift is a symbolic gesture. Going the extra mile by making that symbolism more explicit is a demonstration of thoughtfulness.

**706 Self-theft** "Others are my main concern. When I notice something of mine, I steal it and give it to others."
SHANTIDEVA (7TH CENTURY), INDIA

**707 Give and take** Whenever you buy a new item, give something away. You'll prevent clutter in your house—and in your soul.

**708 Grace** In the Indian healing science of Ayurveda, food that's offered with ill grace or resentment (*bhava dosha*) is more harmful than food that's old and tasteless. When you offer a gift or service, act wholeheartedly, in a true spirit of generosity, rather than merely going through the motions for appearance's sake.

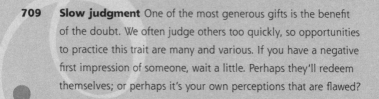

**709** **Slow judgment** One of the most generous gifts is the benefit of the doubt. We often judge others too quickly, so opportunities to practice this trait are many and various. If you have a negative first impression of someone, wait a little. Perhaps they'll redeem themselves; or perhaps it's your own perceptions that are flawed?

**710** **Handover** The presentation of a gift is a richer experience for both giver and receiver if it's handled with grace but without artifice. If you're the giver, resist the temptation to apologize for your offering. If you're the receiver, don't let any doubts about the object itself undermine the sincerity of your gratitude.

**711** **Commendations** When you sense that someone is seeking your approval, commend them if you can do so without betraying your values: this person is obviously feeling vulnerable, and to give them the reassurance they need will cost you nothing.

**712** **Small things** "We cannot do great things on this Earth, only small things with great love."
MOTHER TERESA (1910–1997) ALBANIA/INDIA

**713**    **Good work** Appreciate excellence, no matter how commonplace or small—for example, the workmanship on an old necklace or the satisfying curve on some new fencing. The scope of human talents is vast, and praising achievement gives something back, even when we can't address the person responsible.

**714**    **Specifics** Praise is based on assessment, unless it's automatic—in which case it can hardly be sincere. The recipient will find it rewarding to have at least some details about your reaction. Praising a complex creative project as you might comment on someone's new jacket gives less encouragement than it deserves.

**715**    **Great loan!** Lending something precious—like your car or your apartment—can be more generous than a modest gift. Consider this possibility if you can't think of a suitable present.

**716**    **Congratulations!** Appreciating another's achievement is an important aspect of empathy. Take every opportunity to celebrate success with friends and family. A surprise present needs no better pretext. Feeling another person's joy is a sure sign of a magnanimous spirit, and one that brings its own reward.

**717** **Be prepared** Learn first aid. Knowing what to do to help others if a crisis occurs is a wonderful gift. If you have vulnerable people in your life, such as kids or the elderly, first aid training will also give you the gift of peace of mind.

**718** **Red letter days** In China the color red is associated with good luck and prosperity. Traditionally, a Chinese bride wears a red dress, and any monetary gift is given in a red envelope. Next time you're giving someone a cash gift or voucher, why not make your gift one of good luck as well as money—enclose it in a red envelope to enhance your positive wishes.

# GRATITUDE

**719**  **Thanks plus** Adding a sincere remark or two whenever you say "thank you" for a present or a favor adds flesh to the bones of your appreciation. You might say why you'll find a gift useful, or why it's unexpectedly appropriate. Gushing is merely embarrassing, but a few well-chosen words will reassure your giver that he or she has made a good choice.

**720**  **No limit** Gratitude is a state of mind, not merely a passing response like a sneeze or a smile. This means that it's never too late to mention how appreciative you are of a gift or a service—even if you forgot to send a thank-you card and several months have now passed ...

**721**  **Card store** ... But, of course, you *should* have sent that card: have a supply ready at home. Being able to register your thanks immediately gives a fresh spin to living in the moment.

**722**  **Colleagues** The workplace is a network of cooperative endeavor, and sometimes this can make us take generosity for granted. If someone at work does you an exceptional favor, show

your appreciation. A formal, purchased present might cause embarrassment, but lunch, or homemade cakes or cookies, will help to show that you're feeling grateful.

**723**   **Like and unlike** Fresh flowers are seldom inappropriate as a gesture of thanks—unless, of course, you need to thank someone for a gift of flowers! Ensure that your thank-you gesture doesn't dwarf the thing that prompted it. Morever, it often feels right to choose something different in kind, as well as smaller in scale.

**724**   **Lucky moments** Even agnostics can give thanks for the blessings they receive. Thank God, the One, Fate, Chance, or the First Cause (how you envisage this force or being is entirely your business), or feel a glow of gratitude even if you have nowhere to direct it. The important thing is that you appreciate the fabulous privilege of being alive, now, on Earth, with all the faculties and values you treasure.

**725**   **Happiness x 2** "Gratitude is happiness doubled by wonder."
G.K. CHESTERTON (1874–1936), ENGLAND

# COURAGE

**726**    **Noble knights** Advertise the principles you live by. If you see others breaking your moral precepts, take restorative steps if appropriate, to show by example how you believe people should behave. The age of chivalry may be over, but there's still a place in this world for champions—of truth, fairness, and compassion.

**727**    **Into the fray** We all tend to speak approvingly of erring on the side of caution—especially when we're acting not just for ourselves but collectively for others (our family, our community, our fellow employees). However, there are times when it's right to embark on ventures that will challenge us profoundly. You'll know such turning points when you encounter them—probably from their special chemistry of exhilaration and fear.

**728**    **Dive in** "Pearls do not lie on the seashore. If you desire one, you must dive for it."
ORIENTAL PROVERB

**729**    **Ready for anything** Courage differs from recklessness in coming from a strong, mature assessment. A reckless person has not anticipated the likeliest consequences; a courageous person has, and is ready to face any eventuality that might arise, even the ones that cannot be foreseen.

**730** **Flying leap** To be courageous is to take shortcuts: instead of procrastinating, and pondering all possible outcomes yet again, you take a flying jump ... and land amid the action. You'll only feel lost if you didn't commit wholeheartedly in the first place. Commitment plus courage takes you right where you want to be.

**731** **Siege mentality** Endurance is courage over time. Instead of screwing up your resolve to a sword-point, hunker down for the long siege. Deal with the problems at hand while getting on with other aspects of your life, and stay cheerful, putting others' well-being first. Stick at it: your example will be inspiring to all.

**732**  **River crossing** A major challenge might seem like a river in flood that blocks your path. You can't judge the depth of the water, so you stand there, panicked, wondering what to do. Don't just charge in. Instead, spend a few minutes looking carefully, to see whether stepping stones are visible just below the water's surface. Often they are. Pick your way calmly and carefully. The obstacle may be less formidable than you feared.

**733**  **Light saber** In Aztec mythology, Huitzilopochtli—the god of war—uses the weapon of sunlight to drive away the creatures of darkness (the stars and the moon) from the sky every day. Learn from this warrior of illumination: any time dark or negative thoughts enter your mind, recognize them as your enemy and visualize a sword of bright light chasing them away. Make your mind a sanctuary for sunny, positive thoughts.

**734** **Vigilante** When you sense that others are being treated unfairly, take carefully considered action. Bullying exists in every milieu of life, and it takes a brave soul to stand up to the bully, or to expose injustice to those with the power to act. But you owe it to your values not to be a passive bystander.

**735** **Head first** Plunge into the tasks you've been dreading: there's no better way to prove that your anxieties have been needless.

**736** **Samurai** The Japanese term *bushido*, meaning "way of the warrior," refers to the tradition of respect and devotion between samurai, including absolute loyalty to the master, discipline, self-restraint, and a willingness to sacrifice oneself. Our beliefs in life are likely to be less ritualistic and formalized, and our duty less clear. Even so, bring something of the samurai's dedication to the values you deem to be important.

# TRUTHFULNESS

**737**   **The easy way** Truth is the only approach appropriate to living in the present. Liars have to be mindful of their past lies to be consistent, and this in turn corrupts their future. Avoid all that complication: be truthful. It's much easier.

**738**   **Truth rules** There are three main types of lie: the black lie, which is a downright falsehood motivated by self-interest; the gray lie, which is similar but does no harm to others; and the white lie, which is designed to not hurt people's feelings. Those who believe in the importance of truth will allow themselves to tell only the third type of lie, for the sake of others, and then only after careful consideration: sometimes it's better to be plainly honest.

**739**   **Least resistance** Often we stray from truthfulness simply because we're taking the path of least resistance. It's easiest to say the formulaic things that others say. But language is not merely a tool of social interaction: it's an instrument for discovering and communicating truths, and for sharing experiences. Respect this ideal and your relationships will be more vibrant and rewarding.

**740** **Wakeful** "God offers to every mind its choice between truth and repose. Take which you please—you can never have both."
RALPH WALDO EMERSON (1803–1882), USA

**741** **Bare essentials** In Shakespeare's *All's Well That Ends Well*, a deceitful braggart named Parolles is unmasked as a liar by his army comrades. He vows to himself that he will change his ways. "Simply the thing I am shall make me live," he declares. To strip oneself down to bare essentials is a good way to turn over a new leaf.

**742** **Arrangements** Saying "We must have lunch some time" when you don't really mean it seems harmless. But it can lead you into deeper deception if the other person proposes a more concrete plan. Only make a gesture of friendship if you're willing to follow it through—relationships are too precious to be toyed with.

**743** **Gold standard** "Truth, like gold, is to be obtained not by its growth, but by washing away from it all that is not gold."
LEO TOLSTOY (1828–1910), RUSSIA

**744**   **Excuses, excuses** When we make excuses to others, we often put the true reason second or third in the list, as an afterthought. Be honest with people about why you're unable to do what they ask, or why you've done something that doesn't suit them: this may involve giving more detail than you're used to.

**745**   **On stage** Don't exaggerate the facts for the sake of getting attention—to do service to the moment, you need to be an accurate conveyor of experience. You'll find that describing the nuances is just as compelling as dramatizing the climaxes.

**746**   **Tangled lives** Secrets can be time bombs. If you have a secret, revealing it to anyone creates a network of risk that may trap you at some point in the future. To impose confidentiality on others often just means that you shouldn't be telling them in the first place. The open life, free of secrets, is simplest and happiest.

**747**   **Beyond your control** "If you reveal your secrets to the wind, don't blame the wind for revealing them to the trees."
KAHLIL GIBRAN (1883–1931), LEBANON/USA

## SELFLESSNESS

**748** **Paying in** Every time you make a sacrifice for someone—
whether of time, or money, or opportunity—visualize this as
a deposit into your karmic bank account. Ultimately you gain,
rather than lose, for all karmic deposits earn compound interest.

**749** **Beautiful** "The most sublime act is to set another before you."
WILLIAM BLAKE (1757–1827), ENGLAND

**750** **Renewal** A sense of entitlement, or resentment, or jealousy can
never bring us happiness or esteem. If you find yourself carrying
such emotions, burning like some toxic torch in your heart,
meditate quietly on selfless love. Invite it into your heart
to quench the flame.

**751** **Others first** Small acts of selflessness provide you with good
practice for a compassionate life. Let others take food from
whatever's on offer before you do; share anything you're given
if at all possible; let others decide how you'll jointly spend your
leisure time. Acting as if your claims on life were secondary gives
you privileged membership of a special elite.

**752** **Special restraint** The yogic principle of *brahmacharya* is often translated as celibacy, a loaded concept for Westerners. Modern yogis interpret it to mean not suppression of sexual desire, but instead never directing that desire in a way that leads to jealousy, pain, or conflict. Sexuality is a powerful force, and respecting this fact is essential in spiritual practice.

**753** **The warrior** "I count him braver who overcomes his desires than him who conquers his enemies; for the hardest victory is the victory over the self."
ARISTOTLE (384–322BCE), GREECE

**754** **Charismatic** It's not only assertive people who exude charisma. An attractive aura also emanates from quiet, self-confident people who behave with empathy and intelligence. There's no need to put on an act in social gatherings to be noticed: just open your heart and mind and let grace flow gently into the room.

**755** **Secret saint** Cultivate secret virtues—to be sure that your motives are free of any wish to be admired.

# DETACHMENT

**756** **Rising high** Think of your consciousness as a hot air balloon, lifted by the warmth of your good intentions, but weighed down by past hurts and bitterness. As you fly, visualize a still image of an event that caused you pain, then imagine wrapping it up in brown paper, and throwing it out of the balloon. Watch the past shrink as you rise higher above the ground.

**757** **Arm's length** Emotional attachments can impair our judgment, leading us into self-perpetuating trouble. If you can master the art of emotionally separating yourself from the situations you're in, this can help you with the cool, clear decisions needed to live in a spirit of love, compassion, fairness, and sincerity.

**758** **Under observation** If egotistical urges are pulling you away from the path of goodness, imagine that you're watching every aspect of your behavior on TV—and keeping meticulous notes for reference. Preempt embarrassment by acting well now.

**759** **Bull taming** The principal deity of ancient Persia was Mithra, god of light, who is often shown slaying a bull—which represents the animal passions. If you can conquer the destructive force of lust, then joy, paradoxically, is more likely to come your way. This does not mean a life of abstinence: after all, bulls have their uses.

**760** **No appetite** Fasting (abstention from all or certain foods) is used in many religions as a means of spiritual and physical purification. Fast for a day and accept your hunger as a state of being, like being a Pisces or blonde. Drink only water.

**761** **Freedom** The path of detachment is by no means easy: the shrill voice of emotional need makes itself heard in every area of life. Reward yourself for progress by treasuring each moment of true detachment as a moment of true freedom.

# LOVE AND COMPASSION

**762**    **Touching palms** Energy flows through the body constantly, and touch acts as a conduit for this flow. Touching another person in a spirit of unquestioning, undemanding love creates a two-way healing traffic. Try, for example, touching palms in a "palmist's kiss." Sit facing each other, and press your left palm onto your partner's right palm, your right palm onto his or her left. Close your eyes and visualize the energy flowing between you in a continuous exchange. Feel it cleansing you of all negative emotion—all fear, resentment, frustration, envy.

**763**    **The open heart** Love alerts us to the moment, because even a moment with a loved one can be intensely beautiful and rewarding. A smile, a touch, a reassuring phrase can be a sublime gift. Don't let precious times turn to dust in the gaze of the Gorgon, habit. Be worthy of love and faithfully practice its rites— gestures of attentiveness, empathy, truth, selflessness, respect.

**764**    **Three rules** "Love all, trust a few, do wrong to none."
WILLIAM SHAKESPEARE (1564–1616), ENGLAND

**765**    **Action time** "Practice what you preach" applies to love as well as to moral virtues: it's easier to say the words than to act on them. Agree with your partner to abstain from saying "I love you" to each other for one week, and instead to express your love in action and thought. At the end of your week, you'll find that the words mean more.

**766**    **Love versus power** "Where love rules, there is no will to power; and where power predominates, there love is lacking."
CARL JUNG (1875–1961), SWITZERLAND

**767**  **Out of love** The phrase "falling out of love" implies that love might be a cot or cradle, dangling from a sky hook. It isn't: it's a state of being, and a necessary one. We can't fall out of love: we can only push ourselves. Don't wander too close to the edge of the abyss. Stay safe in the love you found for yourself and your partner. Ignore the ego's demonic promptings.

**768**  **One bird** We all start adult life with an eagle and a dove inside us. The eagle is strong and decisive; the dove is peaceful and nurturing. As we grow in maturity, the two birds coalesce into one. We can act decisively with kindness, we can show strength and gentleness simultaneously. Keep your eagle compassionate and your dove fearless.

**769**  **Your choice** Love has been defined as giving someone that which they need most, even when they deserve it least. Being in love is active, not reactive, and requires a constant commitment toward your partner, even when they're annoying you. It's a tall order—but the passport to a rich life together. Don't let inessentials distract you from the loving path.

**770**   **Happy families** Buddhism teaches that we have each been
reborn countless times since the beginning of creation (in
the cycle of rebirth). This deepens our connection with each
other—in our past lives we may have been siblings. In Buddhist
countries, it's common to refer to other people using the
honorific title of some relative, such as Uncle Teacher. Recognize
the depth of your kinship with everyone, even strangers. That
bond is inestimable.

**771**   **A pure heart** Rising above our emotions helps us to keep our
hearts pure, so that we can spread love and compassion more
generously, without compromise or complication. Love is usually
associated with warmth, and selfishness with coldness, so this
may seem surprising. But relishing your own emotions keeps your
warmth to yourself, whereas observing them with detachment
frees you to be wonderful.

**772**   **The art of gentleness** *Ahimsa* is the yogic practice of nonviolence—one of the five *yamas* (ethical restraints) within the
eight limbs of yoga. It doesn't just mean not being physically

violent toward yourself or others: it also means not having negative, or violent, thoughts, and being gentle and patient at all times. Reflect on *ahimsa* each morning when you wake up and each night before you go to bed—see how much "softer" it makes your life feel to absorb this value into your heart.

**773** **Long-distance call** Our imaginations can visit the most inaccessible places—the molten core of a volcano, the tireless pumping of a human heart. Harness this imaginative capacity to send love where it's needed—into the souls of all living things. You need not try to visualize them all, since the imagination works by symbolism, conjuring the whole from the part. So think of a suitable symbol—perhaps one person in poverty and distress, or perhaps a whole village, seen from above. Then channel your compassion into the symbol—and outward beyond that symbol into the world of the living.

**774**    **Daily wealth** "The days are of most profit to him who acts always in love."

TRADITIONAL JAINIST SAYING, INDIA

**775**    **So many eyes** The peacock is associated in the West with vanity but in the East it tends to be linked with compassion. That's because of the "eyes" in the bird's tail—compassion is all-seeing, a magnificent empathy that notices every need. To be truly compassionate, you must be watchful. Look for telltale signs that indicate when, and how, you can help.

**776**    **Wonderful** "Where there is great love there are always miracles."

WILLA CATHER (1873–1947), USA

**777**    **Empathy and detachment** Being overly empathetic can lead to becoming too involved with, and therefore emotionally dragged down by, other people's problems. Being too detached, on the other hand, might make you distant and unfeeling. Getting just the right balance of the two is the perfect recipe for compassion in action.

**778** **Love is all around** The Buddhist meditative practice of *metta*, or loving-kindness, has four stages. First, the meditator directs loving-kindness toward themselves. Then they switch it toward someone they feel love for already. Next, they transmit the loving-kindness toward someone to whom they feel neutral. And finally toward all beings, everywhere, without distinction. This is the perfect exercise for expanding the heart and finding that the capacity to love is infinite.

**779** **Smallest fellows** In the Eastern religion of Jainism, every living being has a soul: Jain monks and nuns walk barefoot, sweeping the ground ahead to avoid injuring even the tiniest creatures. When insects invade your home, exercise compassion in gently removing them. They too have their role in the wider cosmos.

**780** **Ideal love** "Love is patient, love is kind. It does not envy, it does not boast, it is not proud. It is not rude, it is not self-seeking, it is not easily angered, it keeps no record of wrongs ... It always protects, always trusts, always hopes, always perseveres."
I CORINTHIANS 13:4–7

## SENSE OF HUMOR

**781  Fill your days** "The most wasted of all days is one without laughter."
NICOLAS-SÉBASTIEN ROCH CHAMFORT (1741–1794), FRANCE

**782  Apt laughter** Sometimes we laugh when we don't know how else to behave. Censor yourself if you find that your laughter has turned unkind. Find sunnier sources of humor.

**783  Tidal wave** When something is truly funny, it can be uplifting to let the tide of laughter roar through you and your companions. To be helpless with mirth is cleansing to the soul.

**784  Brighten up your day** "Laughter is the sun that drives winter from the human face."
VICTOR HUGO (1802–1885), FRANCE

**785  Unpretentious** Always look for the humor in your situation. Unless we learn to laugh at ourselves, we will never be completely without delusion.

# 7

## WORLD OF WONDERS

Mind and spirit  294
History  300
Body and self  304
Nature  312
Science and cosmos  326
Experiences  332

# MIND AND SPIRIT

**786** **Mythic quest** Some of the most thrilling stories ever devised, of gods and heroes, are to be found in the great poetic epic *The Odyssey*, composed in ancient Greece by the blind poet Homer more than 2,500 years ago. Odysseus, sailing back to his wife Penelope after the Trojan War, has astonishing encounters with monsters and enchantresses. Read these tales—and invite them into your dreams, for they have an archetypal character rooted in the collective unconscious, that universal pool of imagery we have carried within ourselves since the dawn of history.

**787** **A map of life** William Shakespeare has universal appeal, even today: as Samuel Johnson put it, "His works may be considered a map of life." Some of his plays are grueling tragedies: *King Lear*, for example, shows the terrible consequences of denying familial love. Others are lighthearted comedies, with magic and cross-purposes. See any of them if you get the chance: they are full of vitality, warmth, humor, pathos, wisdom ... and genius.

**788** **Rhyme and reason** Poetry is the opposite of propaganda— it uses words not to narrow our minds but to enlarge them.

It makes us more alert to language. In its traditional forms, it gives us the subliminal satisfaction of rhythm (and often rhyme).

Consider the sonnet, for example: a traditional 14-line form that for centuries poets have used to present "infinite riches in a little room." **Read the sonnets of Shakespeare (789)**, the master of the genre, and decide which is your favorite. Send one as an impromptu e-mail gift to a friend or loved one.

**790** **Mystic insight** Throughout history certain individuals have claimed to enjoy a direct experience of the divine, sometimes unsought, at other times accessed by ritual practices, and have written about their encounters in rapturously beautiful prose or poetry. A prime example is the 13th-century Sufi poet Rumi, who wrote in Persian. He found God dwelling in his own heart. Dip into his great poetry collection, the *Mathnawi*, and be enthralled.

**791** **Waiting for you** The great 19th-century American poet Walt Whitman ends his uplifting *Song of Myself* with one of the most welcoming lines in all literature: "I stop somewhere, waiting for you." Whitman is an inspiring companion. Read his life's work,

*Leaves of Grass*, and be transported by his generous, egalitarian humanity, his plain speech, his openness to wonder and joy.

**792**    **Divine poetry** Many who revere the Judeo-Christian God find parts of the Bible archaic and dry, but some passages are both moving and beautiful. Read the *Song of Songs*, also known as the *Song of Solomon*. This celebrates the relationship between God and his people as a tender courtship and marriage. In the Jewish Sephardic tradition the 117 verses are recited every Friday night. The poetry is unexpectedly sensual—for example: "Your lips drop sweetness as the honeycomb, my bride;/ Milk and honey are under your tongue." Let the poetry enter your heart, and reinforce the message that true spirituality is by no means incompatible with the tenderness of bodily love.

**793**    **Back to basics** There's real wonder in the mind's power as a reasoning tool. Philosophy uses this power to strip away all irrelevance and work out the most basic of meanings from the most basic (and safest) of assumptions. Dip into thinkers like Aristotle, Descartes, and—if you're feeling a bit braver—Kant.

And why not experiment by working out what **your own philosophy (794)** is? Philosophy is the purest use of language, reawakening us to the enigma of being.

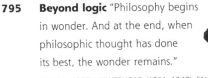

**795**   **Beyond logic** "Philosophy begins in wonder. And at the end, when philosophic thought has done its best, the wonder remains."

ALFRED NORTH WHITEHEAD (1861–1947), ENGLAND

**796**   **Touch of life** God reaching out his hand to touch Adam's, and so giving him the gift of life, in Michelangelo's painted ceiling in the Sistine Chapel, Rome, is one of the most thrilling scenes in all the world's art. No artist has ever captured the potential of a single moment in so dynamic a fashion. In your own creative endeavors, strive for similar moments of electric significance, when a higher power seems to work through you.

**797** **Unique gift** That the likeness of a person can be captured in two dimensions, using merely line and color, is astonishing. When you see a really lifelike portrait, painted or drawn, that seems to capture the life and soul of an individual, reflect on the skills that made it possible, and be thankful for the artist's dedication.

**798** **Gained in translation** "Painting is poetry that is seen rather than felt, and poetry is painting that is felt rather than seen."
LEONARDO DA VINCI (1452–1519), ITALY

**799** **Pure forms** Abstract painting can take us beyond the mundane, recognizable world into an adventure of the mind, questioning the whole basis of reality. Explore the works of some of abstraction's masters, such as Pollock, Mondrian, or Kandinsky— and challenge your assumptions about art and representation. You may find yourself inexplicably moved, even exhilarated.

**800** **Harmonious** "Fine art is that in which the hand, the head, and the heart of man go together."
JOHN RUSKIN (1819–1900), ENGLAND

**801**   **Sacred harmony** From Gregorian chant to Mozart's *Requiem*, sacred music of the European Christian tradition is a sublime expression of faith. Listen to a church or cathedral performance if you can; otherwise, savor a recorded version at night with the lights off, letting the sounds fill the dark room like the voice of the cosmos.

One of many non-Western genres of sacred music worth sampling is **Qawwali (802)**, the Sufi mystic music of the Indian subcontinent, intended to transport both listeners and singers to *wajad*, a state of feeling at one with God.

**803**   **Uplifted** "There is something in music that transcends and unites. This is evident in the sacred music of every community—music that expresses the universal yearning that is shared by people all over the globe."

TENZIN GYATSO, 14TH DALAI LAMA (BORN 1934), TIBET

**804**   **Swingtime** Jazz revels in breaking boundaries, which is precisely what makes it exciting. Get into some jazz grooves, in a club if you can. Marvel at music on the edge.

# HISTORY

**805**    **Speaking volumes** A library, like a chapel, can exude a hushed sacredness—especially one in traditional style with shelf upon shelf of leather-bound volumes. The ancient example at Thebes had an inspiring inscription over the door: "Libraries: the medicine chest of the soul." Find a quiet library and meditate on the healing wisdom accumulated through time—you have your own wisdom to add, even if you choose never to write those insights down.

**806**    **A writer's dream of heaven** "I have always imagined that Paradise will be a kind of library." JORGE LUIS BORGES (1899–1986), ARGENTINA

**807**    **At home** "In any library in the world, I am at home, unselfconscious, still and absorbed."
GERMAINE GREER (BORN 1939), AUSTRALIA

**808**    **Hues of light** The stained-glass window is a beautiful invention of the Gothic style. On a sunny day, the play of tinted light in a shadowy interior is heart-warming—the visual equivalent of heavenly music—while the panes themselves glow with saturated hues. Surrender to such visual harmony whenever you have the opportunity. Light transforming glass is an image of the miraculous spirit transforming a human life.

**809**    **Roots of the present** Ancient sites of ritual, from the stone circles of Northern Europe to the medicine wheels of Native North America, emit powerful but subtle energies. What better places to perform your own personal rituals?—perhaps a rain dance, a prayer for peace, or a thanksgiving for the unfolding of history which makes the present moment flower. At the very least, be alert to the ancient energies of the stones and imbibe the peace in which they have rested for so many centuries.

**810**    **Ancient energies** "Those mossy ancient ruins have not entirely lost their purpose: they feed energy into our nervous systems, keeping us more fully alive."

JEANNE MEUNIER (1846–1920), FRANCE

**811**    **Adventurous soul** In the 13th century, Marco Polo, with his father and uncle, traveled the Silk Road and visited Emperor Kublai Khan, staying in China for 17 years. Polo became an ambassador of the imperial court, writing of his amazing encounters with a vividness that crosses the centuries with ease. No one in history has been more adventurous—until the astronauts of the post-war era. Read *The Travels of Marco Polo* and invite the spirit of adventure into your life.

**812**    **Serene city** Queen of the Adriatic, a city built on the sea, Venice is mystical, melancholy, and achingly beautiful, haunting our imagination. You have only to see a picture of it and it slips into your dreams like a boat down a runway. Once in your lifetime, at least, go on a pilgrimage to St. Mark's Square, and gaze out across the water to the Isola di San Giorgio Maggiore, with its perfect Renaissance church façade and bell tower. Get lost among the bridges and alleyways: you'll be bewitched at every corner.

**813**   **Speaking volumes** "The World is a book, and those who do not travel read only a page."
ST. AUGUSTINE OF HIPPO (354–430), NORTH AFRICA

**814**   **Boy king** The burial mask of the boy pharaoh Tutankhamun, discovered in 1922, is an iconic image of antiquity and a thing of beauty. It's more than 3,000 years old. Look online at a photograph of this marvelous object and project yourself back into ancient Egypt. Imagine the boy king's coronation. History, fully appreciated, feeds wonder into the present moment.

**815**   **Grow up** "To be ignorant of what happened before you were born is to be ever a child. For what is man's lifetime unless the memory of past events is woven with those of earlier times?"
MARCUS TULLIUS CICERO (106–43BCE), ROME

# BODY AND SELF

**816**    **20/20** Those who believe in "intelligent design"—the idea that certain features of nature are so sophisticated that they imply the existence of a Creator—often cite the eye as evidence. Look closely into someone's eye: what you see is the technology of nature—an endless cause for celebration.

**817**    **Nature's handiwork** The way in which cut flesh heals is explained by biology, but it remains an everyday marvel. Compare manmade machines: our bodies are to computers what computers are to hammers—and then some. Look at your hands, flex your fingers, and reflect on the mysterious processes that convert thought to action. We may doubt "intelligent design" but we can't deny nature's miraculous character.

**818**    **To the point** Intuition is a right-brain function that we may never fully understand. Side-stepping reason, intuition shows us that our brains are not just thinking machines, but organs of profound, almost supernatural perception, that "sense" as much as, or more than, they "know." Keep your powers of intuition sharp through the contstant practice of awareness.

**819**   **Myriad selves** Among the human species there's tremendous variation of appearance and physique, even within a single race or family. Similarly, we find infinite variety of character. Rejoice in difference: one of the saddest assumptions we can make is that everyone is pretty much like ourselves.

**820**   **A free gift** Occasionally in our everyday life we'll receive from a stranger a smile that surprises us by its openness and generosity—as if from a heart overflowing with goodwill. Value such smiles as precious gifts—and return them. Smiles bring the beauty of a giving heart to a giving face.

**821**   **Goodwill** "Peace begins with a smile."
MOTHER TERESA (1910–1997), ALBANIA/INDIA

**822**   **Ha ha!** Laughter can be a bond between people enjoying each other's company or a flash enlightening clouds of gloom. It can puncture pretensions we detect in our own attitudes or behavior, and be useful in undermining stale, habitual thought patterns. Use humor as a brush to sweep away the cobwebs of the heart.

**823** **One step back** Grandparents take us one step closer to the roots of our family tree, offering love across the generations. If you have one or more grandparents still alive, and in good health mentally, make the most of this chance to learn directly about your family's past. Ask questions. Celebrate kinship.

**824**   **Marvelous mom** Mothers have a special wisdom: a closeness to what really matters in life. When you speak to a mother, you know she's capable of boundless love. When you're a mother yourself, you know life has given you its most precious gift: a child. Spend time with a new mother and feel her uncompromising love for her baby. She may be stressed at times, but her selflessness reminds us that emotions can be positive as well as negative—and that the transcendence of ego is something that many millions achieve daily.

**825**   **Mother's love** "The heart of a mother is a deep abyss at the bottom of which you will always find forgiveness."
HONORÉ DE BALZAC (1799–1850), FRANCE

**826**   **Birthday bliss** New mothers and fathers feel the wonder of birth more intensely than anyone, but even a non-parent can appreciate the perfection of a baby: focus on the tiny hands, with their tiny fingernails, putting your adult hand alongside for comparison. As Henry David Thoreau said, "Every child begins the world again."

**827** **Couriers of hope** "Every child comes with the message that God is not yet discouraged of man."

RABINDRANATH TAGORE (1861–1941), INDIA

**828** **Down under** For Australian Aboriginals every feature of the landscape has a story to tell, of some incident in the legendary past, a time when ancestral beings wandered far and wide and shaped the land's topography. As an entertainment for children, create your own body of tales linked with your local landscape. Let the kids embroider the tales or conjure up their own. A child's imagination, one of life's wonders, grows stronger if fed with compelling narratives at an early age.

**829** **Fresh thinking** Unafraid to speak their minds, and less susceptible to status anxiety than adults, children have an intuitive wisdom that can get straight to the heart of the matter—often in an amusing way. Make a collection of funny, clever, or wise children's sayings and ponder them from time to time. A child's freshness and spontaneity of thought lie deep within you somewhere: can you resurrect them?

**830**   **Serious fun** "Man is most nearly himself when he achieves the seriousness of a child at play."
HERACLITUS (c.540– c.480BCE), GREECE

**831**   **Peas in a pod** Twins have a mystique about them: in Indo-European myth they are often seen as benefactors or healers. Their empathy is legendary: if one twin trips, both may suffer pain. If you happen to know or meet twins, ask them about their connections and coincidences. Twinship is a marvel of humanity.

**832**   **Beginnings** A birthday is simply an anniversary. But next time you celebrate yours, think beyond the day itself to the actual moment of your entry into the world. Then return yourself to the present by doing, in spirit of self-affirmation, one of the things that's most characteristic of you and makes you special to yourself. Rejoice in your individuality.

**833**   **Perfect sphere** A globe of the world is a representation of the miracle we were born into—a planet which, when seen from space by astronauts, unfailingly inspires love. Spin a globe slowly, as if you yourself were in orbit. Imagine 6.7 billions souls, showing courage, compassion, or forgiveness in countless ways, or suffering in war or poverty. Resolve to help where you can.

**834**    **Golden threads** A city is a phenomenon as unfathomable as our galaxy—all those countless connections and transactions, those mysterious dreams and anxieties, that strangeness and beauty. Uniting all are golden, often invisible, threads of love and compassion—watch carefully for these shining threads as you walk around city streets, and weave your own strands of love for all who cross your path.

**835**    **Word power** The Gospel of John identifies Jesus as the incarnation of the "Logos" (Word), which gives rise to all creation. This ancient idea conferred sacred significance on language. Of course, it's a notion we can intuit for ourselves: whenever we delve into the deepest truths we do so via the ladder of language (even though enlightenment is wordless). Use language with precision and sensitivity, for it's a precious instrument that can guide us on rewarding and exciting adventures.

**836**   **Soul's blood** "Language is the blood of the soul into which thoughts run and out of which they grow."
OLIVER WENDELL HOLMES (1809–1894), USA

**837**   **Articulate** Our language reflects our reality, and the words we use on a daily basis are constantly evolving. Engage with language by listening and learning. When you hear a word you don't immediately know, write it down, and look it up. Words have unique characters, histories, intricacies—and ambiguities.

**838**   **Expand** "Learn a new language and get a new soul."
CZECH PROVERB

**839**   **Inside outside** The mind has an intrinsic paradox: everything we experience outside ourselves is a perception within our heads, while everything inside ourselves is part of the cosmos. It's possible to leap the boundaries: through meditation we can leave our selves behind as we begin to sense, however dimly, the reality of the universe. Our ability to forget ourselves is the greatest power we have, for it's the basis of pure love and true happiness.

# NATURE

**840**    **Small world** A tidepool is a miniature world, often teeming with life, and all the more precious for being temporary. At the seaside, recapture the joys of childhood by finding a weedy tidepool and crouching down to observe its inhabitants going about their business. The middle reaches of the shore have the liveliest pools, with sponges, anemones, worms, snails, crabs and other crustaceans, and even fishes. These creatures live right at the fringes of our everyday concerns: to visit from time to time refreshes our enthusiasm and wonder.

As you **walk along the shore (841)**, reflect on human origins: land animals like ourselves developed from amphibious creatures that evolved in the tidal zone, so without the tides, and therefore without the moon, there would have been no people.

**842**    **Infinite sphere** "Nature is an infinite sphere of which the center is everywhere and the circumference nowhere."
BLAISE PASCAL (1623–1662), FRANCE

**843**    **Pure and simple** Water is vital for life, and the only substance that is commonly found in three different states—ice, water, and vapor. At the symbolic level, water stands for unconscious energy, the formless powers of spirit, and pure nature following its own way without interference (the Tao). Pile ice cubes into a glass and meditate on them till they melt to a pool. This horizontal state of pure being is all the soul is and all the soul needs.

**844**    **Water of life** "When you drink from the stream, remember the spring."
CHINESE PROVERB

**845   Hidden depths** "A lake carries you into recesses of feeling otherwise impenetrable."

WILLIAM WORDSWORTH (1770–1850), ENGLAND

**846   Splash!** Waterfalls, according to Buddhists, represent the "permanent impermanence" of the cosmos. In Japan, followers of the Shinto faith hold waterfalls sacred, and standing beneath one is said to purify the soul. Seek out a waterfall—if possible, bathe in the spray where it tumbles into the waters below. Gravity exerts a tremendous force—without it, there would be no universe. Behold, in the waterfall, the power of gravity made visible.

**847   Appreciation** "Water is the best of all things."

PINDAR (c.522–c.438BCE), GREECE

**848   Back to the source** The journey of the Atlantic salmon from the far wilderness of the ocean back to the river of its own birth and upstream to spawn is one of the wonders of nature, and a fitting emblem of persistence and sacrifice (the trek is exhausting and few survive). Ask yourself what sacrifices will be required of you on your journey through life. Perhaps any suffering you have experienced is part of your destiny?

**849**   **Earthly paradise** The garden is an image of Paradise—an open-air setting in which nature and art are in balance. Any spiritual discipline performed in a garden—yoga, tai chi, meditation, or even prayer—gains from the open air and harmonious environment. Or you can simply relax there, with eyes closed, treating your senses to lovely sounds and smells. **Wind chimes (850)** in a garden add the music of the breeze—gentle, random, and deeply soothing.

**851**   **Difference** "No two gardens are the same. No two days are the same in one garden."
HUGH JOHNSON (BORN 1939), ENGLAND

**852**   **Medley** "We have descended into the garden and caught three hundred slugs. How I love the mixture of the beautiful and the squalid in gardening. It makes it so lifelike."
EVELYN UNDERHILL (1875–1941), ENGLAND

**853** **Wings** Imagine a world without birds—how lifeless it  would seem. Birds rule their own element, delighting us with their beauty—in particular, of plumage and song. They are the natural analogue of angels, and symbolize the links between heaven and earth. When we think of the soul's ecstasy or transcendence, flight is the image we seize upon. Spend time watching birds, through binoculars or with the naked eye, and listen to their glorious songs in the season of courtship. No creatures stir the heart to greater enjoyment: birdwatching, far from being a sublimated form of hunting, offers a true appreciation of wonderful moments in nature. Look out for **homecoming migrants (854)**—celebrate, for example, your first swallow of the summer, rejoicing in its amazing double feat of long-distance flight and accurate navigation.

**855** **A visitation** "I once had a sparrow alight upon my shoulder for a moment, while I was hoeing in a village garden, and I felt that I was more distinguished by that circumstance than I should have been by any epaulet I could have worn."
HENRY DAVID THOREAU (1817–1862), USA

**856**  **Minstrel show** "A bird does not sing because it has an answer. It sings because it has a song."
CHINESE PROVERB

**857**  **Between species** The companionship we humans can share with dogs or horses (and other creatures too) is a testament to our ability to love and communicate beyond intellect, beyond shared interests, and beyond the ties of family. Take time to get to know one or two animals, building a bond of mutual trust. Spiritual kinship outside our peer group brings profound rewards. Animals can be refreshing company, not least in their lack of pretension and their unembarrassed playfulness and affection.

**858**  **Nature lesson** Encourage children you know to explore the beauty of nature. Show them different features, such as buds, caterpillars, lichen, or ants' nests, and explain how one life-form relates to another. Then get the kids to write poems about what they've seen—perhaps in brief, haiku form.

**859**   **Parting gift** Look into the work of the Japanese poet Bashō,
a haiku master, who was able to capture beauty, and express
emotion, in very few words:

> "Dying cricket—
> how full of
> life, his song." BASHŌ (1644–1694), JAPAN

**860**   **Cosmic cow** The cow is a fascinating creature, rich in
associations. Traditionally, crescent horns represent the moon,
while the udder suggests the Milky Way—so the cow combines
lunar and stellar symbolism. To drink cow's milk is an affirmation
of a wonderful symbiotic (mutually beneficial) relationship.
Think of the cow when the world seems all too familiar—its
quintessential strangeness is a tonic for jaded perceptions.

**861**   **Transformation** The development from chrysalis to butterfly is
a potent and universal symbol of personal change—reminding
us that our power to transform ourselves lies within. Butterflies

also suggest the fragile intensity of life's beauty. When you see a butterfly landing on a flower, think of this as all your wishes narrowing to the present to achieve their fulfillment—a perfect awareness of the moment, no less rewarding for being transient.

**862** **Queen of flowers** In beauty, scent, and form the rose is the queen of flowers. Also it has a many-layered symbolism—with connotations of love and sacrifice. Dante compared heavenly love with the heart of a rose, while the Austrian poet Rilke wrote of the petals as the eyelids of a sleepless (eternal) being. Wear a rose sprig in your lapel or in your hat, and pull it out from time to time to relish its beauty and ponder its symbolism.

**863** **A single miracle** "If we could see the miracle of a single flower clearly, our whole life would change."
THE BUDDHA (c.563–c.483BCE), INDIA

**864** **Wise old oak** The oak tree traditionally symbolizes wisdom, strength, and courage. It was regarded by Socrates as an oracle tree, and the Druids ate acorns in preparation for prophesying.

When you next pass an old oak tree, take a moment to consider it in this light. Touch its mighty trunk, or sit under its graceful branches, and absorb its sense of history and wisdom. A little time tapping into its energy in this way may well help you to develop a clearer, braver vision of your own future.

865 **Mountain high** Some might say that the view from a mountain peak is rather like heaven—you worked hard to get there and now you can relax and enjoy it. There are few more rewarding experiences. Next time you climb a mountain or high hill, don't just grab a quick look before heading home again: stay there for an hour (weather permitting) and revel in the airy distances.

866 **Veins in marble** Symbolically, marble is used to denote material or spiritual wealth. If you come across this fabulous stone, look for the pattern of veins, caused by impurities of clay, silt, sand, or iron oxides metamorphosed under intense pressure and heat. Millions of years ago Earth convulsed to bring you this gift for the senses: give thanks to the tide of time for what it brings to the shore of the present.

**White marbles (867)**, such as Carrara from Italy, are particularly prized: the light penetrates a minute distance into the stone before being reflected. The effect gives a lovely realism to sculptures of the human body. Look for such figures in museums of antiquity, and value their brilliance.

868 **Lungs of the planet** The rainforest is a byword for biodiversity, and many of its species, of plant, insect, and animal life, are still unrecorded. It's the planet's natural pharmacy, as well as its lungs and its bestiary. Add your voice to the chorus of protest as the rainforest is cleared by loggers and developers—the health of the planet is measured as much by the fate of the rainforest as of the icecaps.

869 **Winter blossom** There's something strangely moving about the plum tree, which blossoms in late winter, before its leaves appear—as if it were exceptionally eager to please. In the East its flowers symbolize strength triumphing over adversity. In late winter, when you see them, enjoy the contrast of beautiful flowers against bare branches.

**870** **Loveliest leaves** The fall colors are justly celebrated, and in New England there are telephone hotlines that give details of the best locations, scenic drives, optimum viewing dates, and so on. Find glorious leaf hues in fall and reflect on beauty that must always, and without regret, yield its place to the cycle of nature.

**871** **Second spring** "Autumn is a second spring when every leaf is a flower."
ALBERT CAMUS (1913–1960), FRANCE

**872** **Ocean gems** Pearl diving in the South Seas used to be a hazardous operation, which helped to give the pearl its mystique. Not every oyster has its pearl—the "gem" is formed only when a microscopic stowaway infiltrates the mollusk's shell, causing the creature to secrete layers of pearly armor around the irritant. Unsurprisingly, the pearl became a metaphor for something rare and precious. Meditate on a pearl earring or necklace and reflect how beauty is often the accidental result of function—the spirit, for example, when focused on love and compassion, flowering into pearl-like majesty.

**873**   **Heavenly gifts** The ancients believed that crystals fell from heaven as gifts from their ancestors. Rich in symbolism, healing, and poetry, crystals can be used as conduits for the planet's and the body's powerful hidden energies. Buy a crystal pendulum and try your hand at dowsing (see page 332). Or allow the crystals to transform your mood—for example, confidence-building tiger's eye, nurturing rose quartz, or calming amethyst.

**874**   **Natural treasure** The Maya were the first people to cultivate cocoa. It was so important to them that they traded it for other commodities, offered the fruits at festivals in honor of their merchant god Ek Chuah, and gave the beans as precious gifts on occasions such as a child's coming of age. Next time you receive a box of chocolates as a gift, think back to this age when cocoa was so very valuable. Take a moment to appreciate what an amazing natural treasure your simple gift really is.

**875**   **Hidden riches** "The aspects of things that are most important to us are hidden because of their simplicity and familiarity."
LUDWIG WITTGENSTEIN (1889–1951), AUSTRIA/ENGLAND

# SCIENCE AND COSMOS

**876** **Big Bang** The origin of the universe, according to cosmological science, was an outpouring of energy 13.7 billion years ago, out of a miniscule concentration of infinite temperature and infinite density. We can no more grasp this reality than an ant can memorize the Bible: our destiny is to be forever in awe of the ineffable—yet to find transcendence through love and faith.

**877** **Out of nothing** Creationists believe that God created the world. Many scientists subscribe to the idea of the Big Bang. Both views contend that before creation, there was nothing. Could it be that both opinions, in their different ways, are correct? Read the foremost scientists and theologians on the topic of creation—draw your own conclusions.

**878** **Awesome** In the early 20th century Albert Einstein changed our view of space and time with his general theory of relativity. Later came quantum physics and Stephen Hawkings' *A Brief History of Time*. There is no more fascinating intellectual adventure than the continuing scientific attempt to comprehend the universe. Yet each new hypothesis and discovery underlines a timeless truth: the cosmos is a thing of wonder and mystery.

**879** **Fireball** Hard-edged shadows remind us of the wonder of sunlight, which travels more than 90 million miles in perfect straight lines. The sun's yellow color is caused by the scattering of shorter wavelengths of light (violet and blue). When the sun is low in the sky, more light is scattered, causing the color to deepen to orange or red. Next time you see a glowing sunset, bear these facts in mind—your pleasure will be undiminished.

**880** **Splendid silence** "Give me the splendid silent sun with all his beams full-dazzling."
WALT WHITMAN (1819–1892), USA

**881** **Sun worship** In Hinduism, the sun deity Surya is described as the form of god that we see on a daily basis; in ancient Egypt, the sun god Ra was creator of the world and ruler of the skies. The underlying theme is the same: wonder at, and worship of, the sun's immense life-giving power. Sit outside in the sun—feel its glow and marvel at its vitalizing energies.

**882** **Shadow time** Witnessing an eclipse can be an astonishing experience. As the shadow of Earth starts to edge across the sun or the moon, the sheer scale of the phenomenon can be unsettling—as can the realization that our lives depend on a fine cosmic balance. What better time to give thanks for the grand universal system in which we're privileged to have a place.

**883** **Shimmering show** The aurora borealis, or northern lights, is a spectacular, sublime phenomenon of the polar night skies—

a wide curtain of green, blue or red light shimmering like a ghostly theatrical effect. The cause is complex: it results from the reaction of the solar winds with Earth's magnetic field, in certain conditions. If you can, go on a northern lights safari within the Arctic circle, and enjoy the light show of a lifetime.

**884**  **Moondance** In July 1969 two men spent a day on the surface of the moon, then returned safely to Earth. The computer used for this space mission was no bigger than the kind commonly used today in cars: the landing was a tremendous feat of technology and courage. Next time you look at the moon, think of it as a stamp in the passport of civilization.

**885**  **Stargazing** For a shortcut to transcendence, a sky full of stars on a clear night is hard to beat. You need to be away from light pollution: the ideal location is the desert, but any rural area without streetlights will do. In the Northern Hemisphere look for **meteors (886)**, which flare briefly. The most spectacular meteor showers are the Perseids (which peak on August 1) and the Leonids (mid-November).

**887** **Sky view** Next time you look at the moon and stars through a telescope, think of the genius Galileo, for whom the night sky was an adventure, full of potential discoveries. Learn to recognize the most prominent planets, constellations, and star clusters.

**888** **Stardust** "Unknowingly, we plough the dust of stars, blown about us by the wind, and drink the universe in a glass of rain."
IHAB HASSAN (BORN 1925), EGYPT/USA

**889** **Sky lord** When it appears in a clear night sky, the planet Jupiter is easily visible. Two and a half times bigger than all other planets put together, it's brighter than any star, and has a definite disk shape. Its satellite moons are visible through binoculars. As you look at it, reflect on the strangeness of other worlds, and the fact that only familiarity makes our own world less strange.

**890** **Prime time** Numbers have always had their mysterious side: Pythagoras, discovering that musical harmony is based on

simple ratios, concluded that Number animated the universe. Absorb yourself in the properties of numbers— a wonderful labyrinth of abstraction. Of special fascination are prime numbers (indivisible by any number except 1 and itself), such as 11, 601, or 3,797.

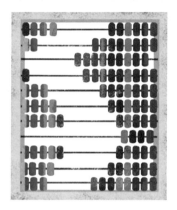

**891** **Same wavelength** The wonder of color is that it can't be described except in terms of the basic vocabulary we've devised for it. We can say something is red, but we can't say what red is like. Color is a primary experience. If spirit is also a primary experience, does that account for why we so often find ourselves unable to explain its significance in our lives?

# EXPERIENCES

**892**     **Elemental scene** The long, straight horizon of the ocean is wonderfully calming—especially in a tropical paradise! It's a good subject for a relaxing visualization. But it's also a reminder of the miracle of the elements—the earth beneath your feet, sky and water dominating your view, and the sun, if you're lucky, blazing upon everything. Relish this elemental experience whenever you get the chance to walk on the shore.

**893**     **Riding high** A brief excursion in a hot air balloon is a popular adventure these days. Take advantage when you find one on offer. Entering the unfamiliar element of air and seeing the landscape from a bird's-eye perspective healthily undermines our habitual modes of perception. And the views can be exhilarating!

**894**     **Hidden treasure** Anyone who doubts the effectiveness of dowsing should reflect on its use in modern times to locate oilfields. Dowsing can be done with an object (not necessarily a crystal) on a string to make a pendulum, a pair of L-shaped rods (which you can fashion by cutting up and bending a metal coat hanger), or a Y-shaped twig (hazel is favored). Ask a friend to bury a metal object or a bottle of water, and experiment. If it fails, change the circumstances and try again. If it works, you have proof that there's more to life than science admits.

**895**   **Spellbound** An 80-year-old man discovers a book of magic spells, and is delighted to find that each one takes a year off his age. After reciting more than half the book, he goes to bed, happy but exhausted. When he wakes next morning, he's eager to get back to his spells but he has a problem: he can no longer read. This simple tale illustrates the power of stories, which appeal to the primal levels of our imagination, and we respond with full attention much as we would have done in antiquity— even when the scenario is so obviously fantastic. Storytelling is one of life's great pleasures. Read the **Arabian Nights (896),** and try spinning tales of your own for children or adults. The storyteller is as important to society as the doctor or judge.

**897**   **Stories** "A book is a garden, an orchard, a storehouse, a party, a company by the way, a counselor, a multitude of counselors."
HENRY WARD BEECHER (1813–1887), USA

**898** **String theory** A violin, when you think about it, is a strange contraption of wood and gut—yet from its bizarre construction expert hands can produce the most exquisite music. Visually, too, these are beautiful instruments. They are analogous, arguably, to the human form—cumbersome in some ways, yet capable of transcendence. Think of lovely string music as the soul's yearning for perfection—and of yourself as an instrument capable of similar beauty if entrusted to the hands of the divine.

**899** **Essential** "Music produces a kind of pleasure which human nature cannot do without."
CONFUCIUS (551–479 BCE), CHINA

**900** **Like the wind** Running is the fastest form of unaided locomotion available to humankind, apart from falling. To be able to run for a mile or more is a skill we should value and exercise, if we can. Fight gravity and inertia; allow your lungs and legs to show their courage. After a good run, lie on the ground and look up at the sky: you'll feel lightly connected to the earth, and conscious of the privilege of being.

**901** **The beautiful game** Competitive activities tend to be anathema to enlightened souls, but are only unhealthy when they are ruthless, embittered, or obsessive. Take chess. The beauty of the game lies in its history, its mixture of complexity and simplicity, the scope it offers for imaginative mental strategies, and its mythic dimension—the dethronement of the king is a theme that constantly recurs in folklore through the ages. There's no better mental workout: choose a well-matched opponent and throw yourself into a competitive dance of the mind.

**902**   **Bananas** Full of vitamins B6 and C and potassium, bananas are health-giving, as well as being wonderfully portable, neat, and in other ways convenient. They could almost have been designed for picnics. Cultivated bananas turn from green to yellow to indicate when they are ripe for eating. Some have cited the banana as a convincing argument for a divinely-made universe— the epitome of "intelligent design." Whatever your beliefs, rejoice in this mini miracle of natural packaging.

**903**   **Geometric magic** The pyramid has long been seen as a supernatural source of energy. Try making your own pyramid, in any material. Plants grown inside an open pyramid are said to be more vigorous in growth, while food kept beneath a pyramid is reputed to stay fresh two or three times longer. Essential oils, herbs, and crystals have been said to gain in power in the same way. People who sleep above small pyramids placed beneath their beds have reported feelings of renewed energy and optimism. All this may sound unlikely—but an open mind will find more rewards in life than a closed one. Experiment— and prepare to be surprised.

**904**    **Daily dosage** Appreciate weather forms. Many are beautiful— snow, sunshine, dawn mist, even rain. Don't get into the habit of treating every day's weather as an irrelevance or a nuisance. We live among the weather of our world and our emotions, and if we are mindful of both, our lives will be enriched.

**905**    **The bright side** "Sunshine is delicious, rain is refreshing, wind braces us up, snow is exhilarating; there is really no such thing as bad weather, only different kinds of good weather." 
JOHN RUSKIN (1819–1900), ENGLAND

**906**    **Storm watch** The weather has its destructive aspect, but a harmless storm, playing across the landscape, is a reminder of elemental vitality. Watch the drama from a safe, dry place whenever you get the chance.

**907**    **Rain blessing** "Many a man curses the rain that falls upon his head, and knows not that it brings abundance to drive away the hunger." 
ST. BASIL THE GREAT (329–379), ASIA MINOR

**908** **White silence** Snow can disrupt, damage, and annoy, but in temperate regions it's often a benign spectral visitor, transforming familiar landscapes. If you can, get out among it: go sledding, even if snow is still falling. As the old saying puts it, "Bad weather always looks worse through a window." After a good snowfall, it's fun to recapture childhood by either tobogganing, throwing snowballs, or lying down on your back in the snow and waving your arms across the surface to make a **snow angel (909)**—a wonderfully pointless gesture, expressing sheer joy in the moment.

**910** **Enchantment** "The first fall of snow is not only an event, it is a magical event. You go to bed in one kind of a world and wake up in another quite different, and if this is not enchantment then where is it to be found?"

J.B. PRIESTLEY (1894–1984), ENGLAND

**911** **Arc of beauty** We always feel fortunate when we see a rainbow—partly on account of its majesty, partly because it tells of sunshine after rain. It's also a heartening symbol of destiny—

the belief that there's a path, even if we cannot know what lies at the end of it. Sometimes we might be lucky enough to see a double rainbow: one arc inside another, with the colors arranged in reverse order. Think of any rainbow as a blessing—the laws of physics translated into a moment of transcendent beauty we can all understand and rejoice in.

**912** **Learned companions** "Will you not open your heart to know, What rainbows teach, and sunsets show?"

RALPH WALDO EMERSON (1803–1882), USA

**913** **Flaky** A snowflake is as precious as a diamond. Its characteristic shape is created by the hexagonal lattice of an ice crystal, branching out into tree-like patterns as it grows unevenly but symmetrically in midair. Each flake consists of billions of water molecules captured from the atmosphere, and some of these will inevitably be from our own exhalations. In a snow shower, let the flakes settle on your coat, and watch their precarious elegance dissolve like the thoughts of the ego fading as you throw yourself into pure perception.

**914** **Breath of being** Song, it has been said, is the breath of humanity responding to its Creator. It can express the whole spectrum of emotions, and arouse the best of them in the listener. In the absence of an instrument, it shows that self-sufficiency can be sublime. Sing of your sorrows and your joys: you can be sure that some songwriter, past or present, has captured your mood to perfection.

**915** **The mediator** "Music is the mediator between the spiritual and the sensual life."
LUDWIG VAN BEETHOVEN (1770–1827), GERMANY

**916** **Not scared** "He who sings scares away his woes."
CERVANTES (1547–1616), SPAIN

**917** **Oasis of graves** Why is it that tombstones and gravestones with age-softened lettering, and maybe a patina of lichen, have something reassuring about them? Perhaps we feel that death, in old cemeteries, has been seasoned by nature, and thus lost some of its bite. These are wonderful places to meditate, or be at peace.

**918**   **Melt away** "For what is it to die, but to stand in the sun
and melt into the wind?"
KAHLIL GIBRAN (1883–1931), LEBANON/USA

**919**   **Universal law** "Death is beautiful when seen to be a law,
and not an accident."
HENRY DAVID THOREAU (1817–1862), USA

**920**   **The deepest question** Philosophy is powerless to answer the
question, "Why is there something rather than nothing?" This
is the mystery of being, self-evident but inexplicable. It's the
enigma we can never confront, because it's forever our dwelling-
place, and we're unable to leave it—nor do we wish to. Think
of this as you scan your surroundings—there's no better way to
reawaken wonder in every moment.

**921**   **Other worlds** It's surely only a matter of time before scientists
discover life on another planet. If we were alone, in an infinite
universe, that would be a miracle. Yet the presence of life
elsewhere would be mind-boggling too. Either way, wonder wins.

# 8

# TOWARD ENLIGHTENMENT

The truth of the spirit  344
Finding your path  348
Faith and belief  354
Beyond mind  366

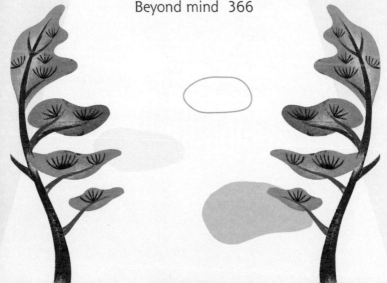

**922**    **Effortless** Think of the path to enlightenment as an act of surrender, not an act of will. The river is already en route to the ocean. All you need do is submit to its inexorable current.

**923**    **Awakening** Imagine that you have petrified into a stone statue. All around you are the spirits of sages, who have visited this world to find someone to carry on their work. Their attention is drawn to the statue, they chip away at the stone, and the crust of inaction and lethargy falls away—revealing you, an awakened being ready for action!

**924**    **Fourfold mixture** For centuries the gods were thought to be cloud-dwellers, and heaven itself has been located in the sky. But to imagine spirituality as ethereal and remote is fundamentally mistaken. Your spirit combines all four elements. It has the fire of passion, and the purifying flames that burn off unwanted trappings of the ego. It has the fluidity of water, molding itself to circumstances. Like air, it is weightless, in the sense of being free of heavy burdens. And, lastly, it keeps its feet firmly on the ground—earth is one of spirit's elements, not its opposite.

**925**   **Reminder of spirit** Your spiritual side may suffer from neglect if you're busy with childcare, or a profession, or simply trying to make ends meet. To give yourself a quick reminder of the deeper things of life, visualize a lotus blossom floating on a pond. Imagine light streaming out from the flower's petals. Let the light fill you with calm radiance and bring harmony back to your life.

**926**   **Open soul** "The windows of my soul I throw
Wide open to the sun."
JOHN GREENLEAF WHITTIER (1807–1892), USA

**927**   **Cup of plenty** The Druids told tales of a bottomless cauldron, whose magic worked through the power of love. Visualize this symbol of the limitless gifts of the universe and imagine it pouring out an endless supply of overflowing, life-enriching waters. Feel the nourishment of this divine irrigation.

**928**   **Light and dark** Battling against darkness is of little use to the seeker. Taking arms against the negative brings the negative into your heart. What you must do instead is let in the light.

**929**     **City of light** In Jewish folklore, access to the radiant city of Luz, one of the seats of the Immortals, lay at the foot of an almond tree. There's a lesson in this: look close to the earth, rather than up in the clouds, for the realm of enlightenment.

**930**     **Perfect circle** The Skeptical thinkers of ancient Greece believed that two propositions could not depend on each other, as that would imply a logical circularity that would undermine the validity of both. In the spiritual realm we need have no such concerns. The existence of love depends on the reality of spirit. The reality of spirit depends on the existence of love. Consider these statements and live by their mirrored truth.

**931**  **Constant truths** "Nothing is secure but life, transition, the energizing spirit."
RALPH WALDO EMERSON (1803–1882), USA

**932**  **Candle in the sun** Ritual and dogma are like candles. They can illuminate part of our darkness when we're stumbling around, trying to find our way; but they can't illuminate *all* our darkness. And when the day dawns, the candle is no longer needed.

**933**  **Empty truth** Go to the quietest place you know—somewhere you can really feel alone. Sit on the ground (or a folding chair), and let your mind and body settle. If there are signs of habitation, imagine them dissolving into empty space; do the same with any landscape features you see. Let them fade until you're left with an experience of emptiness, what Buddhists call *shunyata*. This is not an absence but a presence—profound, invisible, boundless truth.

# FINDING YOUR PATH

**934**  **Truly your own** Finding your path can be difficult, but yogis believe that once you're on it, life becomes simpler and more peaceful. It's advisable not to simply follow someone else's path, for the ultimate result may be *dukkha* (suffering). Ponder your life path. If it feels like it's on loan, it may not be right for you.

**935**  **Magic carpet** To be passive, to have our lives lived for us by our emotions, our attachments, or our ego, is to remain asleep. We may think we're on a path to self-discovery, but that path is completely circular. We are not traveling at all, we're merely fidgeting. Start now to travel adventurously, out of the passive state. Be active and aware, and the path will unfold in front of you like a magic golden carpet.

**936**  **Pathless truth** An illusion to which human beings commonly fall prey is the idea that because we have choices, we are free. As the great teacher Krishnamurti said, "Truth is a pathless land." Choices are not the same as discoveries, for discoveries come from stillness and silence, not from an exertion of the will. So long as we choose, we're still trapped behind the veil of illusion.

**937**    **Becoming the path** "You cannot tread the path until you become the path yourself."
ZEN SAYING

**938**    **Roadblocks** Patañjali lists nine obstacles that we have to overcome in our quest for freedom (*kaivalyam*: illness, lethargy, doubt, impatience, fatigue, distraction, arrogance, inability to take a fresh step, and loss of confidence). When these obstacles occur, they cause negative thinking or physical discomfort. When you doubt yourself or feel distracted, ask yourself if one of these obstacles is in your path. If so, work gently to remove it.

**939**    **Parable** In the narrow crowded streets of a town in North India, an elephant was blocking the way to market. No one knew how to get by the beast. Then the townspeople saw a holy man walking down the street. "If anyone knows what to do, he will," they said to each other. When they looked again, the guru had vanished. A few minutes later, when they looked toward the elephant, they saw him beyond the elephant, approaching the market stalls. He had simply made a detour around the block.

**940**  **Support systems** The mind is like a creeper plant, which needs support to help it grow healthily, with purpose; without this support, it may wander aimlessly or out of control. Indian philosophy teaches us to cultivate self-support in the form of spiritual exploration, dedication, and discipline.

**941**  **Commanding the winds** You can shout at the wind to enter your house; you can pin a notice on a tree trunk, commanding the wind to come inside. Neither approach will work. But there is another, more effective way: simply leave your window open.

**942**  **Fourfold way** In the *Bhagavad-Gita*, written 2,500 years ago, the Lord Krishna instructs the warrior Arjuna in four different approaches to life: knowledge (*jnana yoga*), devotion (*bhakti yoga*), right action (*karma yoga*), and meditation (*raja yoga*). These are the building blocks of your inner abode. Your four walls won't have equal numbers of each type of brick—there will be a patchwork of types, whose precise composition depends on your temperament. Find the approach that suits you and follow where it leads. Switch to another way if that seems intuitively better.

**943**    **Enlightenment's enemy** In Buddhism, the demon Mara personifies the passions that ensnare us. During the night of the Buddha's enlightenment, Mara appears in various guises: first his beautiful, seductive daughters appear to tempt the Buddha, then hordes of slavering beasts descend to terrify him. Through both trials, the Buddha sits unmoved and refuses to give up his seat to Mara. As the morning comes, the Buddha reaches enlightenment. When you're suffering through a dark night of the soul, reflect on this tale. Identify in your own heart the manifestations of Mara, and see if you can banish them as the Buddha did.

**944**    **Spiritual humility** Modern New Age writers often emphasize the omnipotence of the awakened self: the spirit within gives us vast reserves of power, we're told, and no human achievement possible on this Earth should be automatically ruled out. It's true that most of us have more talent than we recognize. Yet we must not lose our humility: the time-honored sin of pride exists in a spiritual as well as a material version. Spirit is the potential for greatness, but true greatness has roots in modesty. Self-esteem is not the same as self-importance.

**945** **Same difference** The spiritual seeker might well ask lots of questions. Is there a difference between awareness and enlightenment? Is it a matter of degree? How will I know when I'm enlightened? Each question of this kind you put to yourself or to others takes you one step backward on the road to enlightenment. Truth is not the answer to a question.

**946** **The wanderer** In India the term *parivrajaka* is used to describe a wandering, mendicant monk. Unburdened by possessions and cravings, his spirit is free. Ask yourself if, in your heart, you are a *parivrajaka*, even though in your outer life you have a home and possessions. Think of these as ephemeral, disposable, spiritually worthless. This way, when you see where the path to enlightenment might lie, you'll be well-equipped to explore it.

**947** **Silent witness** Once we've begun to see that the self is distinct from its thoughts, its sensations, and its experiences, we start to be less anxious about mortality. As death approaches, we are the witnessing spirit, and because the spirit transcends the body, the witnessing will go with us when we pass away. That notion

is the source of all true faith. According to Buddhism, those who have access to that source are the enlightened ones, the Buddhas.

**948**   **Overflowing** Keep an open mind as you set off on your path. A professor went to a Zen master called Nan-in to learn the art of Zen. Nan-in served him tea but kept on pouring when his cup was full. The professor protested, "No more will go in!" "Like this cup," answered Nan-in, "you are so full of your opinions and ideas. I cannot show you Zen unless you first empty your cup."

# FAITH AND BELIEF

**949**    **Double-sided** Fear of change, or of deepening truth, or simply a fearful attitude to life, can all hinder us on the journey to enlightenment. The opposite of total fear is total faith—like a coin that's finished spinning, one side is always uppermost in our practice. It's natural to feel a sense of trepidation, but whenever you feel fearful, let go and have faith in your chosen path.

**950**    **Lonely twin** "Doubt is a pain too lonely to know that faith is his twin brother."

KAHLIL GIBRAN (1883–1931), LEBANON/USA

**951**    **Perfect circle** In Buddhism, the auspicious symbol of an eight-spoked wheel represents the Buddha's teachings (the *dharma*). The circle symbolizes the perfection of the teachings, while the spokes refer to the Noble Eightfold Path (see page 121). Read some of the Buddha's discourses, which are both poetic and inspiring. Can you absorb some of his wisdom into your life?

**952**    **Seeing and believing** Seeing is believing, it's sometimes said. But seeing is in fact a more primary experience, and believing

is often little more than a kind of mental embellishment—
something we wear, without having a deep experience of its
value. To be enlightened is to see, with absolute clarity. Once
we progress from believing in God to seeing God, we take a
major step forward on our path.

**953**    **Manifestation** "Faith is to believe what you do not see;
the reward of faith is to see what you believe."
ST. AUGUSTINE OF HIPPO (354–430), ASIA MINOR

**954**    **Falling well** Many people struggle intellectually to find some
solid ground for their belief in God or the Spirit. Letting go of
such inner conflict might be the first step toward resolving it.
After all, we don't need to believe in the law of gravity to drop
a coin into a needy person's hand: all it takes is action driven by
love, and the coin falls. There's nothing to worry about: just keep
up the good works.

**955**    **Inner knowing** "Listen and attend with the ear of your heart."
ST. BENEDICT (c.480–c.547), ITALY

**956** **Three-legged friend** In Celtic tradition the triskele is an important symbol—three running legs or spirals curving out from a central point, like uncoiling springs. Meditate on the triskele (above) and draw on its energy to help you through times of challenge, change, and doubt. Focus on each spiral in turn and allow it to awaken your dormant faith in yourself.

**957** **A true companion** Belief in where we're headed is our most important trusted ally on the spiritual path, fighting off the dual enemies of complacency about past success and despair at how far we still have to go. Put trust in your faith, and lean on it when you need to: as Patañjali says, "Faith gives us the energy to achieve success against all odds."

**958** **Hand in hand** "Strong faith brings happiness. We feel at home in our lives and in touch with something larger."
JOAN DUNCAN OLIVER (BORN 1944), USA

**959** **Bright faith** The blind faith of habitual thinking, which causes us to accept dogma unquestioningly, is the opposite of "bright faith," which is based on an inspiring teacher or teaching. Bright faith can start us off with hope and determination on the road to enlightenment. En route we'll probably have doubts. But if we're fortunate, we'll also have experiences that confirm our faith.

**960** **The three qualities** Traditional Zen training deemed three qualities necessary in a student: great faith, great doubt, and great effort. Imagine yourself as dedicated to your path as a Zen student. Don't forget that to doubt doesn't mean to fail: it may just be another step on your journey toward faith.

**961** **Ties of spirit** The word *religion* derives from the Latin *religare*, meaning "to bind"—a phrase with implications of community. Religious beliefs can be divisive, but if we go deeper than doctrine we find not division but unity. Faith in the divine links us not only with all those who believe as we do but with all souls everywhere. Feel a sense of this spiritual kinship.

**962** **Conundrums** Encountering difficulties in our spiritual quest can be challenging, but remember: puzzling our way through life's metaphysical and moral conundrums is one of the things that defines us as human. Take comfort—we all struggle sometimes.

**963** **Matter of choice** In religious lore we often come across the notion of chosen people, selected by God for salvation. According to modern spiritual thinking, salvation comes to those who choose themselves, not directly but indirectly—by choosing others as the recipients of their love and care.

**964** **The big picture** "Unity in variety is the plan of the universe."
SWAMI VIVEKANANDA (1863–1902), INDIA

**965**   **Myriad seeds** The scriptures, of various
religions, offer their wisdom in the
form of countless insights. What
are we to do with these? One
answer is to treat these words
of wisdom as seeds, which you
need to plant in the fertile soil
of the heart. There they will grow
and create a divine garden within
yourself. Here you will spend
your happiest hours.

**966**   **Good books** The scriptures
of different faiths are both
a fascinating introduction
to the world religions, and
an illuminating source of
knowledge on the universal
values. Study these texts,
even for a short time, and

absorb their essential messages and fascinating stories. What do they tell you about humanity, about faith, about yourself?

If reading the whole of the Bible or the Koran seems like an impossible task, **dip in at random (967),** and pick out a sentence or a few lines. Trace their relevance to your life. Maybe there's a message for you here, however indirect.

**968** **Silent teacher** Reading a book of spiritual wisdom is not like reading a book of history or political analysis—you're not simply absorbing information, you're spending time in the enlightened company of a sage. Appreciate the character and values of the author, as well as their explicit insights. Get to know them as people. Some of the most powerful lessons they have for you might be hidden between the lines.

**969** **Learn by heart** Take the wisest words of the wisest teachers deep into your heart, and honor them there. Don't allow them to become clichés. Regularly remind yourself of the words, and remember their intention. Where you can, carry these wise words into action in your own life.

**970**  **Aspects of God** Some mystics see every awakened human being as an aspect of the Divine. Self-exploration and deep introspection have acted for many people as portals to profound spiritual truth. Explore the possibilities: to find divinity within is to discover the true wonder of human experience.

**971**  **Divine path** "I've had enough of my own dream—
I want to walk in God's."
ALAIN (1868–1951), FRANCE

**972**  **Behind the veil** On your path to enlightenment your thoughts will often turn to the Divine. Approach the concept with as few preconceptions as you can. The first one to shed is the idea that God, like the Greek deity Zeus, has human characteristics. Some of the obstacles to belief, such as the question, Why should God tolerate the existence of evil, or withhold proof of his existence, disappear once this notion is abandoned. Build your own view of the Divine, based on intuition, with help from mystic literature. But remember that words are a chasm, not a bridge: you will only perceive God in wordless silence.

**973**    **Visitation** "You know, God does visit us. A lot. It's just that most of the time we're not at home."
ANONYMOUS

**974**    **Offering up** The yogic precept *isvara-pranidhana* means surrender to a higher power: *isvara*, which can be translated as "God," or the source of knowledge, or simply something that gives total clarity. Consider this idea of surrendering your actions to a higher power—not passively, but by being more alert to the intention and effect of everything you do.

**975**    **All-seeing** Imagine God is looking at you through a telescope from heaven. What appeals to him about you? What repels him? What does he think about your life's strategy? Does he know anything about you that you don't know?

**976**    **Cosmic dance** The three main Hindu gods represent the three phases of life: Shiva is the destroyer, while Brahman creates life, and Vishnu preserves it. But Shiva is often represented in his form of Nataraj, or Lord of the Dance, symbolizing the

continual cycle of creation and destruction. Balanced on one foot on a prostrate figure representing ignorance and illusion, he is surrounded as he perpetually dances by fire, snakes, and skulls, symbols of this endless cycle. Find a picture of Shiva (online perhaps) or acquire your own small-scale figurine (they are quite common). Contemplate the rhythmic movement and tranquility simultaneously present in the image.

977 **Prayer to Allah** "O Lord! Increase my astonishment of You!"
BAHA'I PRAYER, PERSIA

978 **Dressage** A thoroughbred horse is said to need only a gentle touch of the whip to know exactly what his master requires of him. It's the same with enlightenment. A soul with well-developed awareness on the path to nirvana needs only the lightest of suggestions from a teacher—perhaps a Zen koan (paradoxical parable), perhaps a line from the *Tao te Ching*, perhaps a glance at the smiling face of the Buddha—to do the right thing. Like that horse, be watchful and responsive. And don't try to gallop to enlightenment: you're bound to stumble.

**979**   **Be present** "Absolute attention is prayer."

ZEN SAYING

**980**   **Health spa** The sacred atmosphere in buildings used for worship can be very moving, whether you're religiously inclined or not. Churches, in particular, are good places to think or to meditate— especially if they have stained glass, which can cast a wonderfully transcendent light into an interior. If you're lucky, a choir may be practicing, adding the dimension of heavenly, echoey voices. Don't expect a spiritual flash of illumination—just treat the place as a health spa for the soul. If you prefer the outdooors, prehistoric stone circles can be used to similar effect.

**981**   **Real improvement** "Who rises from prayer a better man, his prayer is answered."

GEORGE MEREDITH (1828–1909), ENGLAND

# BEYOND MIND

**982**    **Through the keyhole** The unenlightened soul looks at existence, the cosmos, everything, through a keyhole. A form might pass by—a person, an animal, a vehicle, a rain cloud— and we merely glimpse it as it passes. Enlightenment, achievable through profound meditation, admits us through the keyhole into the true nature of the cosmos. Your view will be partial until you broaden your vision by accessing the spirit and the One.

**983**    **No reasoning** "Truth never argues. It is a song, not a syllogism." OSHO (1931–1990), INDIA

**984**    **The silent observer** According to yoga, our perception is made up of two elements: *purusa* and *prakriti*. *Purusa* is our pure internal consciousness, the part of ourselves that "watches" all our actions, while *prakriti* is everything external: our bodies, matter, and the universe itself. We see the truth clearly with our *purusa*, but it's clouded by habit and false understanding, and we confuse our true "selves" with external things, such as our bodies or possessions. Only the constant practice of awareness can separate *purusa* and *prakriti*, and help us toward clear thinking.

**985**     **Bare floors** The house of enlightenment is a place without cushions. Until we attain awareness we use mental cushions to protect us from reality. Only about 2 percent of experience filters through to us. Awareness brings much more experience within our scope, and we live happily in an uncushioned abode, with bare floors and no illusions. Once we attain enlightenment, an extraordinary insight dawns: we see that the comfortless, bare-walled interior is a heavenly palace.

**986**     **No change** "Before enlightenment I chopped wood and carried water; after enlightenment I chopped wood and carried water."
ZEN SAYING

**987**     **Without monkeys** Speak to yourself the following phrase: "A forest without monkeys." Although the forest has no monkeys, it's almost impossible not to imagine them: the very word "monkeys" summons them in your imagination. When you can imagine a forest truly without monkeys, you'll have become enlightened. Forget about the monkeys and let the forest rise in your being like love or peace.

**988**  **Once again awaken** "Regain your senses, call yourself back, and once again awaken. Now you understand that only dreams were troubling you, regard this so-called reality as you regard your dreams."

MARCUS AURELIUS (121–180), ROME

**989**  **Intuitive seeing** Parmenides, an ancient Greek philosopher, believed that the reality of the world is "One Being," an unchanging, eternal, indestructible whole. This is *aletheia*, or Truth. According to Parmenides, movement and change are merely appearances of this static, eternal reality, which we can access by Reason. In fact, it's more rewarding to see reality as a fully integrated whole, in which movement and change and eternity coexist without contradiction. To perceive this truth, reason indeed offers us a lens—but of what use is the lens of reason without the eye of awareness?

**990**  **Eternal source** "All things come out of the One and the One out of all things."

HERACLITUS (c.540–c.480BCE), GREECE

**991**    **Goldfish** A profound Buddhist symbol is
the golden fish, whose movements reflect
the enlightened person's ability to move freely
and fearlessly in any direction. In an unenlightened
state we're landlocked, surrounded by the unreachable
waters of the spirit. Boats—the various artificial means
we may seize upon to attain salvation—provide only a
temporary solution. However, enlightenment gives us the
freedom of a new element, a new dimension: we can swim
in the swirling currents of Oneness.

**992**    **Spiritual geometry** The sage and teacher Prajnanpad, among
others, has spoken of opening out the ego. Eventually it becomes
a gigantic circle, admitting all reality, a circle so vast that its
circumference becomes infinitely extended—into a straight line.

**993**    **Rainbow truths** A rainbow, we might imagine, gives the basic
ingredients of any color—except for gold and silver. All we
imagine can never be all there is. The enlightened mind knows
both the beauty of the rainbow and its limitations.

**994**    **Pole sitter** In a Zen koan (paradoxical parable) a master asked the question, "How does someone sitting on top of a hundred-foot pole step forward?" They might believe that they've reached enlightenment after profound meditation; but unless they know how to step forward in the ten directions, they haven't. Ponder how this can be done. This is no trick question: it's simply that words and logic cannot help us reach nirvana.

**995**    **Bell and thunder** In Tantric Buddhism the bell symbolizes the truth of emptiness, while the "diamond thunderbolt" symbolizes the spiritual path. Let the bell of emptiness sound inside yourself: to perceive emptiness, the underlying perfection that lies within all forms, is to experience the lightning flash of revelation.

**996**    **The narrow gate** "Every second of time is the narrow gate through which enlightenment might enter."
MODERN INSPIRATION FROM BEIJING

**997**    **Ox herding** In the 12th century, Zen-minded spiritual seekers used the ten Ox-Herding Pictures to help them find enlightenment. The ox is a symbol of our true nature. The scenes shown are as follows: a man is looking for his ox, he finds footprints, he glimpses the ox, then manages (just) to hang on to it, then tames it, then rides it home happily. In the seventh picture there's no ox, only the man. In the eighth image, an empty circle, the man has vanished too. In the ninth we see pure landscape. In the tenth, the man, barefoot, "enters the marketplace with giving hands." Inner wisdom has enabled us to forget the self, see the world as it is, and reenter the community of souls to participate helpfully in its joys and sorrows. Ponder the sequence, and follow it in your life.

**998**    **Masculine, feminine** Eckhart Tolle has described, in *The Power of Now*, how women tend to be closer to enlightenment than men. That's why the Tao is described by Lao Tzu in female terms, as "infinite, eternally present, the mother of the universe." Masculine "mind energy" is hard and focused; feminine "being energy" is soft and inclusive. Men who find their hidden reserves of being energy will find that new pathways open up inside themselves. Women who let their "being energy" pour forth unhindered, without trying to emulate male focus, will blossom into their true, loving, questing selves.

**999** **Music and silence** Consider what is truly constant and then, by contrast, what is endlessly changing. Both these opposites are to be found within the one cosmos, the one lifetime—ours. Embrace the constancy as God and the changeableness as God's countless manifestations in life.

**1000** **Just be** "Salvation is in the truth and in being."
ALAIN (1868–1951), FRANCE

**1001** **Unfolding creation** Many sages find it limiting to think of creation as either the Big Bang or a one-off project by God. Whatever your religious beliefs, you'll perhaps find a more dynamic view of creation more appealing. If the material world is endless change, then creation is an ongoing process. Our selves, our destinies, are being created constantly through our thoughts and actions. Attune yourself to the inherent creativity of your life. Let enlightenment be the finishing touch on your masterpiece.

# INDEX *The index refers to page numbers, not numbered points*

acceptance 257, 258, 260, 261

achievement 74, 221

acquisitiveness 64–5, 81

acting 77

acts of kindness 156–8, 160–61, 162, 163

acupressure 173

Advaita Vedanta 204

adventure 302

Aeschylus 48

affirmations 18, 72, 115, 192

aging 47–9, 50–51

Alain 361, 373

alarm clocks 210–11

alchemy 89

Alcott, Amos Bronson 208

alertness 16, 217

alphabet, spelling 135–6

altruism 163

ambition 254

Amiel, Henri Frédéric 225

ancient sites 73, 301–2, 365

anger 25, 108–9

animals 63, 165, 318, 319
   imagining oneself as/ imitating 100, 221

anniversaries 264–5
   see also birthdays

anxiety see worry

Apollinaire, Guillaume 212

apologies 262

appearance 71

appreciation 142
   see also gratitude

archetypes 228, 294

Aristotle 80, 258, 280, 296

aromatherapy 67

arrangements 277

attachment(s) 196, 281

attention 16, 21–2, 32–4, 36–9, 84
   body and 168
   and exercise 31–2
   see also focus

"attraction, law of" 198

audits 32, 87, 124–5, 143

Augustine of Hippo 303, 355

Aurobindo, Sri 205

aurora borealis 328–9

awareness 8–11, 26, 82, 191, 367
   intuition and 304
   inward/outward 190
   love and 88
   mindfulness and 36
   movement and 86
   of others 146

Ayurveda 265

babies 139–40, 307

Bacon, Francis 44, 196

balance 125, 126, 202

balloons, riding in 332

Balzac, Honoré de 307

bananas 336

Barrie, J.M. 163

Bashō 319

Basil of Caesarea 337

baths 226

beauty 81, 209

Beecher, Henry Ward 333

Beethoven, Ludwig van 340

being and nothingness 341

belief(s) 75, 76–7, 79, 80, 111, 192, 258–9
   "law of attraction" 198

Benedict of Nursia 151, 355

betrayal 262

*Bhagavad-Gita*, the 350

Bible, the 51, 290, 296, 310

Big Bang 326–7, 373

birds 316–18

birth 307

birthdays 48, 149, 264–5, 309

birthstones 198–9

Blake, William 279

boats 241

body 26–8, 40, 41, 176

body image 71

body language 103–4

body wisdom 104, 175

books 161, 186, 300–301, 333, 359–60
   see also reading

Borges, Jorge Luis 300
boundaries 148, 311
brainstorming 45
bravery see courage
breathing 38–9, 40, 84,
173–5, 176, 183–4
bee breath 184
breath mantra 185
dragon's breath 223
sun breath 173
Buddha, the 16, 70, 76–7,
86, 137, 152, 181, 320
Buddhism 21, 49, 287, 354,
371
Eightfold Path 84, 121,
252–3, 354
Four Noble Truths 121
see also Dhammapada
and Zen
bullying 275
Bushido 275
butterflies 319–20

Cage, John 65
Cameron, Julia 46
campaigning 160
Camus, Albert 324
candles 39, 152, 180–81,
347
Carlyle, Thomas 67
cat exercises 100, 221
caution 272

celibacy 280
cell phones 8, 127
cemeteries 340
ceremony 18–19, 139, 301
Cervantes, Miguel de 340
chakras 41, 62, 112, 195
challenging 275
Chamfort, Nicolas-Sébastien
Roch 291
chance 59
change 20, 58–9, 89–93,
243, 261, 319–20, 373
decisions concerning 95
noticing 33
worry and 119
see also under habit
chanting 112–13, 184–5
charisma 280
charities 160, 165
chess 335
Chesterton, G.K. 52, 271
chi 172, 174, 198, 234
children/childhood 139–40,
141–2, 165, 307–9,
312, 318
chocolate 325
choice 55, 348
chores 32, 208
Chuang Tzu 201
churches 365
Cicero, Marcus Tullius 303
circadian rhythms 211

cities 310
civility 158, 165
clothing 199
clutter 159, 198, 265
cognitive behavioral therapy
192
coincidences 56
cold calling 165
collections 308
color 41, 61, 212, 230–31,
269, 331
flower coloring experiment
140–41
commemoration 138
commitment 273
communication 21–2, 23,
103–4, 132–6, 276
massage 67
community 130, 156–65,
309–310
commuting 214
comparison 146
compassion 120, 165, 285,
287, 288, 289–90
compliments 114, 131, 143
computers 225, 304
concentration 37–8, 84–5,
224
see also attention and focus
conditioning 77–8
confidentiality 278
Confucius 76, 87, 334

consolation/comfort 73
constancy 373
consumption 81
contentment 257–8
  see also happiness
contradiction 71–2, 80
conundrums 254, 358
conversation 21–2, 133–5,
  148
correctness 74
courage 123, 272–5, 280
covetousness
  see acquisitiveness
Coward, Noël 143
Cowper, William 186
cows 319
creation 326–7, 373
creativity 43, 44–6, 55,
  297, 373
crises 269, 351
criticism 77, 143
crystals 61, 325
curiosity see questioning
cycle, existence as 47
cycling 174

Daedalus 254
Dalai Lama 299
dance 31
Dante Alighieri 320
darkness 231, 347
day, looking back on 227,
  231
  see also diary-writing

de Mello, Anthony 88
death/dying 123, 340–41,
  352
decision making 75, 94–5,
  116, 224, 254
  in families 141
de-cluttering 159, 193, 198
decorations 162
delegation 127
delusion 9, 70
denial 191
dependence/independence
  see independence
Descartes, René 296
Desikachar, T.K.V. 204–5
desires 64–5
destiny 55–6, 57, 198
  see also fate
detachment 38, 281–2, 289
Dhammapada, the 25, 88,
  110, 113
diary-writing 23, 44–6, 114,
  228
  analysis 114
Dickinson, Emily 22
difference 74, 146, 315
digestion 216
discovery 241
DIY 233, 239
Dōgen 257
doodling 46
doors 232–3
dowsing 325, 332–3
dreams 228–30

drinks 217, 226, 235–6, 319
driving 214–15
Dryden, John 96
duality 204–5

earth 309–310
  see also environmental
    issues
Eckhart, Meister 85, 264
eclipses 205, 328
ecstasy 261
Edgeworth, Maria 14
Edison, Thomas 79
Einstein, Albert 19, 327
electricity 101
e-mail 8, 136
Emerson, Ralph Waldo 21,
  62, 139, 158, 209,
  240, 277, 339, 347
emotions 9, 107–114
  feelings and 107–8
empathy 289, 291
emptiness 49, 347
endurance 273
energies 195, 336
  see also chakras and chi
enlightenment 10, 344, 346,
  352, 364, 366–7,
  369–73
entertaining 34, 148.150–53
enthusiasm 59, 60
environmental issues 159,
  161, 162, 322
Erasmus, Desiderius 55

essential oils 66–7
eternity 22
ethics 163–5, 250–55, 259–60, 272
see also environmental issues
evolution 313
excuses 278
exercise 31–2, 126, 174–5, 235, 238
see also running, swimming, and walking
exercises 215, 216, 217, 221–2
see also under breathing
exorcism exercise 111
experience, unrepeatability 102
explanations 262
extremes 258
eyes 178, 217, 304

faith 90–91, 354–5, 356–7
family 137–42, 306–8
fasting 212, 282
fate 52, 260
see also destiny
fear 102, 110, 198, 354
feelings 107–8
see also emotions
feet 30

feng shui 198, 230–31, 232–3, 234
fire 40, 92–3
"fire in belly" 40
first aid 269
fishing for compliments 114
flowers 320, 322
coloring experiment 140–41
focus 21–2, 37–8, 39
position and 27
see also attention
food 34, 212–13, 215–16, 234–7, 243, 246, 336
forgiveness 24, 25, 262–3
form and emptiness 49
fractals 201
Frankl, Victor 120
Franklin, Benjamin 99, 118, 247
Freud, Sigmund 228
friendship 131, 148–9, 176–7, 216–17
fundamentalism 259
future, thinking about 6, 52–3, 196

Galileo Galilei 330
games 335
Gandhi, Mahatma 264
gardens 35, 315
gender 202, 372–3
gibberish 42
Gibran, Kahlil 278, 341, 354

Gide, André 53
gifts/giving 153, 162, 163, 264–5, 266, 268–9
as daily duty 164
giving away objects 159, 161, 162
as thanks 271
Gladstone, William 217
God 43, 85, 361, 362, 373
Goethe, Johann Wolfgang von 233
grace 265
grace before meals 236–7
Graham, Martha 31
grandparents 306
gratitude/thanks 23, 145, 152, 153, 154–5, 165, 208, 212, 236, 270–71
gravestones 340
group meditation 39
grudges 262
guessing 103
guests see visits
guilt 115
Gyatso, Tenzin 299

habit(s)/routine 9, 87, 96–102, 208, 227
changing/varying 31, 33, 34, 96–102
haiku 318–19
hand positions/gestures 18–19, 181–3

happiness 55, 57, 62, 81, 197, 233, 260, 311
  ethics and 132, 163, 250, 279
  gratitude and 271
  habit and 102
  seeking 30, 110
  sharing 152
  trying to repeat 102
  work and 220
  see also contentment and joy
harvest 245
Hassan, Ihab 330
Hawking, Stephen 327
health/healing 209, 304
heart 94, 112–13, 176
heat and cold 258
hedonism 6
heirlooms 137
Heraclitus 205, 309, 368
Herodotus 50
Hesse, Hermann 134
hidden aspects 325
Hildegard of Bingen 43
hindsight 51
Hinduism 164, 204, 362–4
history 301–3
hobbies 238
holding on 14
holidays see vacations
Holmes, Oliver Wendell 135, 311
home 32, 230–31, 232–4

Homer 294
honesty 276–8
hot air balloons 332
Hubbard, Elbert 220, 256
Hugo, Victor 291
humility 254
humming 184
humor 291, 305
  see also laughter
Huxley, Aldous 102

Icarus 254
identity see self
ignorance 76
Illich, Ivan 178
illusion 204
imagination 78, 308
impermanence 49
incense 29, 67
independence/dependence 8, 52, 95, 101, 174, 190, 239, 260
individuality 146, 309
information, human implications 130
inner refuge 61, 120
insects 290, 319–20
inspiration 59–60
instinct see intuition
"intelligent design" 304
interests 238–9
intuition 25, 103, 304
irritations 257

Jainism 290
James, Henry 219
James, William 79, 243
jazz 299
jealousy 279, 280
Jerome, Jerome K. 57
jewels and jewelry 198–9
Johnson, Hugh 315
Johnson, Samuel 101, 294
Joubert, Joseph 46, 57
journal-writing see diary-writing
journeys 179, 190
joy 197, 282
  see also happiness
judgment 266
Jung, Carl 56, 131, 228, 284
justice 18
justifying 77

Kafka, Franz 261
Kant, Immanuel 296
karma 130, 250, 253, 279
Kenn, Thomas 211
Kierkegaard, Søren 51
kindness, acts of 156–8, 160–61, 162, 163
King, Jr., Martin Luther 90, 177
Kipling, Rudyard 62
Krishnamurti, Jiddu 348

La Fontaine, Jean de 149
landscape 195, 200, 308
Langer, Ellen 96

language 276, 310–311
  philosophy and 297
languages, learning 242, 311
Lao Tzu 200, 372
laughter 259, 291, 305
"law of attraction" 198
Lawrence, D.H. 37
learning 48, 76, 130, 154–5,
  195, 256
  see also teaching/teachers
leaves 246, 324
leisure 238–43
lending 268
Leonardo da Vinci 298
Leopardi, Giacomo 142
letters 23, 136
letting go 90, 262
libraries 300–301
life 341
light see darkness and sun
lightness 79, 193, 259, 260
limitations 55
listening 15, 134, 176
  to music 239–40
lists 32, 126
litter 159
logic 346–7
losing oneself 190
loss 122, 138, 149
lotus flower 64, 196, 256,
  345
love 24, 25, 34, 88, 284–5,
  287, 289, 290, 311
  fear and 110

instinct and 25
meditation 279, 288, 290
  power and 284
  spirit and 347
luck 58, 87, 137
lust 282
lying 276

machines 119
Maeterlinck, Maurice 110
mandalas 49, 188
mantras 18, 86, 184–5
maps, walking without 190
marble 321–2
Marcus Aurelius 89, 94, 368
Mary Stuart 132
massage 30, 66, 67
meditation 9–10, 18–19, 27,
  84–5, 180–89, 311
  group 39
  incense and 29
  as inner sanctuary 61
  loving-kindness 290
  movement and 86, 186
  observing thoughts in 38,
    180, 193
  sound/silence and 67
memories 6, 14, 104–5
memory 16, 22, 105–6, 303
Meredith, George 365
metaphor 43–4
Meunier, Jeanne 302
microcosm 201
Middle Way 53

Milarepa, Jetsun 180
mind 36, 37–8, 311
mindfulness 6, 10, 26, 84, 86
  awareness and 36
  exercises in 14–15, 38
  position and 27
misfortune 120, 122, 243,
    260
  laughing at/taking lightly
    259, 260
  see also suffering
Miyazawa, Kenji 120
Montaigne, Michel de 116
moon 187, 329, 330
morning 208, 209, 210–11,
    212–13
motherhood 140, 307
motivation 60, 87
mountains 175, 321
movement 27, 86
  see also exercise
moving on 90, 262
mudras 18–19, 181–3
music 239–40, 299, 334, 340
mysticism 295

nature 18, 61–2, 92, 196,
    226, 257, 304, 312–32
  energies in 195, 200
  see also seasons
    and weather
negativity 345
neighbors 156–60
New Year 246–7

[ 379 ]

Nietzsche, Friedrich 74, 175, 231
Nin, Anaïs 95
no, saying 20, 62–3
noise 65
non-action 18, 19
nonviolence 287–8
northern lights 328–9
nostalgia 104, 196
novelty 32
now 6, 14, 16, 191
numbers 148, 330–31

obituaries 155
objects 34
    see also possessions
observation 14–15, 16
ocean 312–13, 332
Odysseus 294
oils 66–7
Okakura, Kakuzō 111, 219
Oliver, Joan Duncan 357
"om" 184–5
openness 259
opinions 80
    see also belief(s)
Oppenheim, James 30
opportunities 20, 57, 165, 191, 224
organizing 159, 160
Osho 366
Osler, William 221
others first 279

otherworld 226
outdoors, time spent 209, 244–5
overflowing cup 353
Ovid 59

painting 298
Pancatantra, the 120
Parmenides 368
parties 156
Pascal, Blaise 313
past
    attitudes to 104–5
    describing 108
Patañjali 39, 91, 257, 349, 357
path, finding 348–9
patience 257, 260–61
peace 269, 305
pearls 324
peer pressure 146
penitence 115
perception 197
Perls, Fritz 228
perseverance 256
philosophy 296–7, 341
photographs 138
Pilates 171
pilgrimage 179, 202
Pindar 314
Pine, Albert 159
place 195, 200, 308
planning 32, 90–91, 124–6
    daily 209, 211

telling others about 99
platitudes 133, 276
Plato 240, 260
play 309
Plutarch 34, 90
poetry 43, 55, 294–5, 298, 318–19
Polgar, Alfred 125
politeness 158, 165
Polo, Marco 302
positive psychology 163
positive thinking 191
possessions 159, 161, 162, 265, 352
possibilities
    see opportunities
potential 63–4
poverty 81
power 351
practice 189, 238, 257, 304
praise 143, 268–9
    see also compliments
Prajnanpad, Swami 191, 369
prayer 365
pregnancy 139
presents see gifts
Priestley, J.B. 338
priorities 124–7
    see also time
        management/use
problems, separating 109–111
procrastination 127
productivity 221

projects 223, 238
protection 56, 199
Proust, Marcel 145, 241
public speaking 41, 160
punctuality 220
purification 151
purpose 126
pyramids 336
Pythagoras 330–31

Qawwali 299
Quakers 177
quarrels 24, 25
questioning 19, 70, 74–5,
    85, 87, 192, 255

Rāhula 256
rain 337
rainbows 338–9, 369
rangoli 150
reading 37–8, 46, 230, 333
    see also books
reality 70–71, 205, 368
reason 94, 104, 205, 304
reassurance 266
recycling 161
regrets 56–7
relationships 10, 23–5,
    81, 86–7, 131, 132,
    135,143–9, 262, 277,
    284–5
  age and 51
  at work 225, 270–71
  auditing 143

interests and 74–5
  problems with 143,
      144, 262–3
  see also community,
      conversation, and
      family
relaxation 238
religion 259, 358, 359–60
resentment 25, 262, 279
respect 22
responsibility 141, 252
rest 230
restitution 115
Rilke, Rainer Maria 320
risk 52, 53, 95
ritual 18–19, 301
role play 144
routine see habit
Rubin, Theodore Isaac 60
Rumi 295
running 334
Ruskin, John 298, 337

sacrifice 279, 314–15
safety 53
Sai Baba 178
sailing 241
salvation 358, 373
samurai 275
sanctuary 61, 120, 230–31
sand mandalas 49
satsang 255
scale 200
scallop shells 202

scent 28–9, 66–7
Schopenhauer, Arthur 122
science 205, 326–7
seaside 312–13, 332
seasons 244–7, 322–4
secrets 278
security 347
self 33–4, 81, 82, 131, 193,
    252
  changing 91
  forgetting 311
  victory over 110
self-doubt 71–3
self-esteem 72–3, 225, 227,
    351
self-examination 199, 251,
    256
self-image 75, 77, 78, 105
self-knowledge 80, 108
self-massage 30, 66
self-presentation 77, 78–9
self-punishment 115
self-realization 204
self-reliance/self-sufficiency
    see independence
selflessness 279–80
Seneca 58, 123, 127, 165,
    243
sexuality 280
Shakespeare, William 197,
    260, 277, 284, 294,
    295
shamans 121
"shanti" 185

Shantideva 265
sharing 152
Shaw, George Bernard 224
shells 202
shiatsu 173–4
shopping 81
short-termism 125
silence 66, 85, 176,
    177–8
  in communication 133,
    134, 135, 176–7
similes 43–4
simplicity 18, 19, 63–4, 65,
    95, 254, 325
singing 340
sitting 27, 186
skill(s) 21, 56, 238–9
sharing 142
  volunteering 160
sleep 47, 227, 230, 231
  consciousness as 88, 205
small things 266
smell see scent
smiling 192, 305
snow 338, 339
society 146
  see also community
Socrates 18, 320
solstices 73, 244
songs 15
  see also singing
Sophocles 52
sound 42, 65
space 62

speeches 41
spelling alphabet 135–6
spend-free days 214
spiritual 10, 344–5, 346–7,
    351–3, 358
sporting events 131
stained glass 301, 365
stars and planets 226,
    329–30
Steinbeck, John 243
stone circles 365
storms 337
  calm in 178–9
storytelling 333
strangers
  empathy with 164
  helping 156–8, 160–61,
    162
  politeness to 158, 165
stubbornness 75
success 74
suffering 49, 120–23
Sufism 26–7
sun 210, 226, 244, 264,
    327–8
support systems 73, 350
surrender 344
swapping 163
swimming 174–5, 226
symbols 56, 201,
    202, 256,
    320, 338–9, 356, 369
  in dreams 228
synchronicity 56

Tagore, Rabindranath 308
tai chi 9, 172
talismans 56, 199, 202
talking sticks 135
Taoism 18, 63–4, 364
Tarot, the 199
tea(s) 217, 219, 226, 246
tea ceremony 219
teaching/teachers 60, 142,
    154–5, 318, 360
  see also learning
technology 8, 101, 119
teenagers 142
  see also youth
telephone 135–6, 216–17
Teresa, Mother 266, 305
texts, carrying 214
Thackeray, William
  Makepeace 65, 78
thanks/gratitude
  see gratitude
thinking 79
Thoreau, Henry David 25, 66,
    81, 90, 197, 307, 316,
    341
thoughts
  effects 89, 90, 92
  as fiction 88
  labeling 193
  language and 311
  rejecting 193
  watching 38, 180, 193
tidepools 312
tidiness 233